How We Became

Camille Moore

Dedication

This book is dedicated to our past experiences, Our Present Self and the opportunity to become who we were destined to be.

The Holloway Sisters

"Well, this is it." Honey Holloway closed her suitcase and zipped it as she motioned for her fiancé, Jared Maxwell, to remove it from the bed and set it at the front door.

"Have you already called your taxi?" he asked.

But she hadn't. The truth is she wasn't ready to make this trip. She sat on the bed staring out the window of the New York City loft she was fortunate enough to love her way into several years ago. Didn't really seem as though it had been that long since she had met and fallen in love with this wonderful man who had accepted her flightiness and unfocused passion for life and loved her in spite of herself.

Honey had moved to New York from Cleveland, Ohio, right after high school to study dance at the Dance Theater of Harlem. It had always been her passion, even when her father told her how she would never make it as a dancer—she was too clumsy and she moved awkwardly, unlike the swans you see in ballets. Some days she believed it, too, but Diane, her middle sister, would always tell her not to listen to that fool, that he didn't know what he was talking about and that she was just as beautiful and graceful as any dancer who ever floated across a stage.

She practiced hard her whole life, even took a good beating for it sometimes, as did her mother, Josephine, for spending what her father called his hard-earned money on nonsense that wouldn't amount to much of anything in the future. Sometimes Josephine would even sneak and go clean a house with her friend Mabel, who had a small cleaning business she was trying to start. She would leave the house in a nice dress and act as if she was going to lunch or out shopping with Mabel or to play cards, but she would go straight to Mabel's house, change clothes and scrub floors so Honey could dance and Jim her husband would be none the wiser.

It was worth it to see Honey grow up and dance all over the world, which was what she'd spent all of her twenties doing, and she'd loved it. Jared was the only thing she'd found that even came close. She met him when she was twenty-seven at a friend's birthday party, and other than her touring, they had been inseparable. He was the reason she decided it was time to stick closer to home just a little more, and that was how Flight, her dance studio, came to pass. Her skills, his knowledge of business and not to mention a little money he had saved, made her vision a reality. A vision she may have never had without him. If Honey hadn't met Jared, she'd probably have died an old woman in a small Harlem apartment, still trying to go out for auditions. Sad but true.

Her sister Diane was totally different. She was stern, determined and fought for the things she wanted in life and was not going to be told no at any cost. She was four years Honey's senior, and even though she was the middle child, she was always the boss and was always the leader. Even June Marie, who was the oldest, knew Diane was the boss, and at an early age ceded that title to her.

Diane took care of everything and everyone and held it all together. Honey couldn't wait to see her. She missed her so much. The three sisters talked on the phone, except during June's brief hiatus, and emailed and were as much a part of one another's lives as if they lived down the street from one another, but they weren't that lucky. June Marie had run off to LA with her musician boyfriend when she was twenty-one. Their mother was sick for weeks, not because she missed her, which she did, but because she ran off with her musician boyfriend. She had always talked about becoming a nurse, but when Charlie came along and put it on her, she was gone.

After a few days of partying, which in reality was more like five years, she woke up one morning with her man passed out under her arm and a woman she barely remembered meeting the night before across her leg and the smell of unsuccess lingering in their one-bedroom Hollywood apartment. This was not the glamorous life she'd dreamed of when she put her suitcase in the car trunk of one of Cleveland's best keyboardists and hit the highway for a five-day road trip. He made good money playing backup on people's albums and touring, but most of it went on clothes, cars and eating in fancy restaurants, trying to prove they belonged in L.A. The rest went up their noses.

That day, June crawled from under the half-naked woman, and it was the first time since she had gotten on that roller coaster ride that she felt embarrassed by who she had become. She quietly tipped into the shower, attempting to wash away the last few years of her life as she looked up at the ceiling and asked God to get her out of this mess she had created. The tears began to stream down her face, and she sank down into the shower and wept for who knows how long before pulling herself together as best she could and calling her friend Jill. If she was gonna get better, she couldn't do it with Charlie. He didn't think there was anything wrong with their lives, and she wasn't going to waste her breath trying to convince him there was.

After packing a few necessities, she wrote Charlie a short note that simply explained she had lost her way and had to go so she might find her way back. She explained she loved him very much, but she needed a different life and would never ask him to change for her or give up the music he so loved.

Withdrawal was horrible and hard. She craved the white substance that had become her friend. She had no idea she had actually become a real addict because even past her casual use, it had always been readily available, so she never knew what it was like to want it and it not be there until that period in her life, and she was mad. Mad at Charlie, mad at the world, but most of all mad at herself for becoming this person who had lost so much in such a short period. She was strong though—all the sisters were. Each displayed their strength in different ways, but nevertheless, strength was a character trait each of them possessed.

Diane stuck around Cleveland as long as she could bear, mainly because she had to make sure Honey was okay. Once Honey left for New York, that was her ticket to ride. She was always smart and had gone to college and then on to law school. She had pondered staying when she finished school and practicing law there, but there was so much social inequality looming in the South, far greater than the North, so she headed to Georgia to become the great Black savior. That Diane, you didn't want to get on her bad side. She fought for the rights of Blacks any way she could—landed in jail twice; almost got disbarred; and had her house egged, spray painted and who knows what else, but it never stopped her from fighting for the cause of the moment. It use to scare Josephine, but someone had to do it. Everyone couldn't just sit idly by. Everyone talked about change back then, but few stepped up to the plate to make change happen. People had their reasons for not stepping up, which ranged from fear to complacency, and Diane possessed neither.

These three sisters each have a story of their own, which we will delve into later, but this weekend, they would all see one another in the place they had so desperately run from. They had no choice. Mother had suddenly become ill, but the doctors couldn't really explain it. Some say life will do that to you sometimes, just make you not want to live it anymore. No one specific thing happens, just the accumulation of life's events. That's probably what happened to Josephine Lilly in that season of her life. She just realized she no longer wanted to participate, at least not on this side of glory, as the old folks would say. Walking out of the grocery store pushing her cart, she just stopped and sat down right on the concrete that hot, humid August afternoon and slowly fell over on her side. A young man saw her and frantically tried to revive her, asking if she was okay while a young lady ran into the store to call 911. The paramedics arrived on the scene and began CPR. Just as quickly and easily as she was gone, she was back. She looked up into the paramedic's face and asked, "Why did you do that?"

"Do what, ma'am?" He was confused.

"Why did you bring me back?" She sighed a long, deep sigh. "I was on my way home. I was almost there. I could see the trees. They were so green, and the water was like a blue I'd never seen, so beautiful you can't describe it, and I was at peace. I didn't have a care. I was getting ready to step down onto the lush green grass, and you ruined it. You brought me back here."

The paramedic apologized and chalked it up as her being a little old and a little delusional—or maybe just having passed out due to the heat or possibly fatigue. Nonetheless, he paid little attention to it and got her on to the hospital.

After a thorough examination and several tests, the doctors could find absolutely nothing wrong with her. Her health was fine, she wasn't dehydrated, and her blood pressure was fine. You name it, they checked it, but there was nothing to be found. They kept her overnight for observation and until all her bloodwork was back and she was sent home. Though the doctors could find nothing, Josephine knew there was nothing left here for her. She was tired and decided she was ready to go. She had lived, attempted to love, brought forth life into an angry world, saw that life grow and depart from her. Her part was complete. Life had been bittersweet for Josephine, but she took the bitter with the sweet, and in spite of it all, she found a way to remain sweet. It's not like she was that old, but she was old enough, and not even the thought of her grandchildren could keep her here.

This, however, was enough to bring the girls a runnin'. One thing they loved more than one another was their mother. She had been such a valiant woman. Always loving, always sweet, always giving—sometimes a little too much. She had done an awesome job raising the three girls and the last addition, Jim Junior, who had come along two years after Honey. Especially after losing their father. Jim Junior was not exactly all she hoped he would be but he was hers, and she never spoke ill of him. The girls, however, saw him a little differently.

Josephine called each of them on the telephone one by one and told them not to be alarmed but she'd had a minor incident, had spent the night in the hospital and was now home and feeling just fine. But she didn't feel just fine. Every time she closed her eyes, she'd hope to open them and no longer be there. Depression did not seem to be haunting her, at least she didn't think so. She was just done, finished, and felt any additional day on this earth was pointless.

Home Again

T he sisters each arrived at the house, one by one, Diane being the first to get there. She pulled into the driveway remembering how proud they were when they'd moved into this suburban house. She remembered she was twelve, June Marie was thirteen, and one thing they definitely were was mad. Yes, they were happy to have this big pretty house in the suburbs because that's the reaction they were told by everyone they were to have, but that meant leaving the only neighborhood and friends they had ever known to live in a place where they really weren't wanted. This was 1967, and the living wasn't easy for Blacks, especially Blacks who didn't want to settle for living in the inner cities or even in the areas that were nice, but still just for Blacks. They had to leave the comfort of their friends and start over at a new school, where there would likely be few Blacks, if any. How could they be expected to do that? It just wasn't fair by any stretch of the imagination.

Shoot, the only thing that halfway saved them is the fact they were pretty, just like their mother. That's one of the reasons Jim liked her. For as dark as his skin was, hers was that much lighter. Josephine always said she was the closest thing to a White woman he was going to get.

Diane and June heard that several times come across their mother's lips, never in front of Jim, but usually after he had brought her home a certain dress to wear out or after he would coach her on what he expected her to say and how he expected her to act while they were out in public, so as not to embarrass him. This was crazy because she spoke proper English—no slang was ever allowed in the house in front of her—and she carried herself like the beautiful lady she was. The girls were raised the same, so ladylike. Josephine believed these things were important in those days if you were going to get ahead in life.

Jim was a factory worker in an automobile plant, but he knew how to save money, and he was a dreamer. The only problem was the big dreams inched along for a Black man, and though he had some success, the dreams never came to pass the way he saw them in his mind, and he always seemed to take it out on Josephine, whom he called Lilly. Maybe Josephine wasn't quite White enough or well-connected enough for him. Whatever the case, if things were not right for him, they were going to be horrible for her.

The memories that begin to flood Diane's mind as she walked through the back door were almost too much to bear. She remembered standing on that very step listening to her father berate her mother, comparing her to the women on television who kept a perfect house and raised perfect children all while looking good at all times and never being too tired to sex their man after his long day at the office. Diane could never figure out why her mother put up with him as long as she did. She pushed the memory from her head and took in the aroma of fresh-baked biscuits coming from the kitchen.

"Hey, Momma." She ran and threw her arms around Josephine and held her.

"Alright, alright, that is enough. Stop making such a fuss." Josephine wiggled her way loose.

But deep inside Josephine's heart, she was so excited to see Diane. Her heart did a little somersault. After all, she had not seen her since last Christmas.

"Okay, Momma. What's going on here? No one passes out when there's nothing wrong. I mean, were you dehydrated, were you dizzy, what exactly happened?"

"Diane honey, I do not want to talk about it right now and have to keep retelling it. Let's just wait until your sisters get here and we can all sit down and talk, okay? Just give me that."

She had to put it that way because the lawyer in Diane would just keep drilling away as if they were in a courtroom and Josephine was on the stand avoiding questions.

Diane relented and agreed to wait. "Yes, Mother," she said in a jokingly sarcastic voice, "I understand. It can wait. But these biscuits can't." She walked over, grabbed a biscuit and began to butter it up. "Do you need me to do anything?"

"No." Josephine sighed. "Everything is under control in here." She smiled and looked pleased with Diane.

Diane was stuffing the highly buttered biscuit in her mouth when Honey came running through the door screaming, almost knocking her over.

"Dee, I missed you so much. It seems like forever. I can't believe we are all going to be here at the old house together. It's crazy, right?"

"Honey." Diane hugged her back. "You know I hate when you call me Dee. It's Diane."

Honey blew her off. "You'll always be my Dee. I'm not calling you Diane, so you might as well stop telling me to. Has it worked so far?" She cut her eyes and walked over and kissed Josephine.

"My little Honey, just so grown up and beautiful. Seems just like yesterday we were bringing you home from the hospital. Stand back, let me have a look at you. Turn around."

Honey did a pirouette, showing off her dance skills. Josephine loved to see her dance. She would come to New York now and again when Honey still danced in productions.

The Way It Is

Poor Honey almost didn't make it into the world. Jim had wanted a boy so bad to carry on his name. His friend Bobby would tease him about not being able to make boys after the girls were born, not knowing how much of a sore spot this was for Jim. Josephine had a miscarriage and one baby who was stillborn between Diane and Honey, and at that point Jim didn't want any more children. He would blame Josephine for not giving him a son—told her there was something wrong with her body and her eggs were no good. When she got pregnant with Honey, he told her to get rid of the baby. He didn't want another mouth to feed and more dresses to buy—their house had enough women—but Josephine refused. She was not raised that way. There was no way she could kill an innocent unborn baby, a gift from God, so Jim decided he was going to beat it out of her. She took her beating from Jim as she had to do from time to time to keep a roof over her children's head and food in their little bellies.

"You not keepin' that baby, Lilly. You just not."

"Now, Jim, how can you expect me to kill this baby? That is not what God would want from us."

"Do not try and bring God into this. God also wants you to listen to your husband, and I said we are not having no more kids in this house."

Josephine touched Jim's arm. "Jim honey, please, I am begging you. Don't be like this. We will be fine."

"Be like what?" The statement enraged him. "Be like what? What am I being like? Huh?"

He swiftly slapped her to the ground. "What's wrong with how I am, huh? Like you so much better than me."

Josephine looked up at him. "Please, Jim," she begged. "That is not what I meant. I was…"

He kicked her as she attempted to get up, and the scene played out as it had many times before.

He beat her pretty bad that day. She didn't get out the bed for two days. Diane and June knew something was wrong. They just didn't know what. Every time Diane questioned Jim about Josephine, he would tell her to mind her business. June sat outside the bedroom pleading with Josephine to open the door. She refused in a soft, pleasant voice, assuring June everything was fine and that she was just a little under the weather, but they knew better. They had seen Josephine get a smack here and there, and sometimes they could hear them arguing, but nothing prepared them for the day their mother came out of that bedroom black, blue, purple and red. Her attempt at camouflaging with make-up was extremely unsuccessful. One of her eyes was swollen shut, her mouth was busted, and her arms had Jim's fingerprints embedded in them. She smiled through her pain and embarrassment, asking them what they wanted for breakfast as if nothing was wrong. Their father sat at the kitchen table reading his paper and drinking his coffee as if he saw nothing wrong with her. They began to cry and asked if she was okay and what happened.

"She's fine. Now go on and get ready for school before you're late," he barked, never looking up from his paper.

He stood, folded his paper and kissed her on the cheek.

"I think the abortion would have been a little less painful. No way your baby still in there. Fix yourself up before I get home. I don't wanna see you like this. Put some more makeup on or something."

"You did this?" Diane cried out. "I hate you! I hate you! Why did you do this? You're a monster."

"Diane, that's enough," Josephine called out to her. "Come on now, calm down."

"You want a dose? You not gonna disrespect me in my house. You hear me?" He lunged as if he were going to come after her."

Josephine pushed Diane behind her. "Go ahead on now, Jim, before you are late. She will be fine."

He turned to leave, slamming the door behind him.

Little Honey survived that awful beating and two more after that, and finally Josephine convinced him the baby was meant to be there. She even gave him the hopes of it being the son he longed for, but when it wasn't, it just made it that much harder on her and Honey. Jim wouldn't even hold her. The only thing he did for Honey was provide food, shelter, clothing and criticism. June was by far his favorite. He doted over her, and Diane ran a close second, but Honey would never know the love of her father, so she withdrew and was a little mousy when she spoke, but when she danced, there was power like you'd never seen, and that was her escape. He would go to her recitals and school performances, but only to keep up appearances. If people knew what really went on in that house, they would look at him so differently, so he would make sure that would never happen. When Josephine would be healing from bruises, he would tell people at church or neighbors she was down south visiting family or wasn't feeling well. People liked Jim—the Jim they knew—and he dared anyone in that house to let on any different.

Jim was a confident, good-looking Black man. Some people were afraid of real dark men at that time, especially if they were big in addition to being Black, but Jim was tall, slender and well built. He could have modeled with the pretty boys, suave debonair men of his time if only he wasn't Black. But people loved him, his charming personality and charismatic smile, which was hard not to be drawn in to. He was born in Mississippi the third of eight children, and being one of the oldest brings responsibility you don't even ask for, but when you were living under your parents' roof, you did as Ruth and Chester said. He saw his father work early days into the night sometimes, and they never seemed to have enough. His mother cleaned houses during the week and did other people's laundry on the weekends so it was almost as if the children were raising themselves, but they were smart, resourceful and Jim got in his head he was gonna find a better life when he got older. He watched his parents work themselves nearly to the grave and have nothing to show for it. Times seemed to be slowly changing everywhere except the South.

He made up his mind early on he was gonna be somebody. He was going to have everything the White man told him he was excluded from. He longed for the day to not have to stand by while someone berated him because of the color of his skin. Standing in front of the store waiting for his mother to come out, he looked through the window just waiting, hoping she would hurry up. He only came because he would have to help her carry the bags home. This man rubbed his mother's butt with his hand, and he watched his mother tense up. He couldn't hear what the man was saying to her, but then he grabbed her crotch through her dress, and when she tried to push his hand away, he spit on her. Jim ran through the door and charged at the man who grabbed him, and his words tore through Jim.

"What cha gon' do, boy? You better git cha colored self from out of here before I kill you."

Jim responded, "I'm gonna tell my daddy."

The man laughed. "Tell yo' daddy, and what's he gonna do, watch me have yo' momma? If you and yo' daddy know what's good for ya, you'd do wise to remember ya place." He groped Jim's mother one last time and laughed as he walked out the door.

The rage burned through him. "Momma, what we gon' do? He can't just do that. We gotta get 'im." There were tears in his eyes and hers.

"It's gonna be alright, Jim. Don't worry about things you got no control over. The sooner you learn that, the better off you'll be. Some things is just the way they are, and ain't nothin' you can do 'bout it."

But Jim could not just go along with that. What did she mean some things are the way they are? What did that mean? He couldn't wrap his little nine-year-old mind around that. That day it meant it was okay for another man besides his daddy to touch his momma. He soon learned it meant that and so much more.

When they arrived home, Jim took the groceries in then came back outside and sat on the front porch waiting anxiously for his father to return that day to tell him what had happened. The longer he sat, the madder he got. Finally, he saw the top of his father's hat coming up the road, and he ran out to meet him. He was out of breath and frantic as he attempted to tell his dad what had transpired that day.

"Whoa, slow down." Chester chuckled, not realizing the gravity of the situation Jim was attempting to relay. Jim bent over to catch his breath, started from the beginning, and told his father the whole story, right down to the man grabbing his mother's private parts and laughing.

"Well?" He looked up at his father, waiting for something—anything.

"Well, what?" his dad responded verbally while another piece of him slowly died due to the color of his skin and the way the world viewed it. He couldn't let Jim see this. He wanted his son to be able to grow up in this world that hated him without getting himself killed, and in the 1930s South, this was a hard thing to do.

"Well, what chu gon' do?"

He stopped walking. "What do you want me to do, Jim? Huh? You want me to go get myself killed defending yo' momma's honor? Is that what you want? Then who's gonna take care of you and your brothers and sisters? Yo' momma will be alright. Ain't like she ain't never been touched down there before. Jim, you gotta learn some things just ain't worth dyin' for. You gotta use ya head."

"But, Daddy, he spit on her, too. You gotta do somethin', don't cha? I think she wanted to cry, Daddy. She just didn't. I could tell she wanted to. She didn't want him touchin' her."

Jim's father bowed his head in cowardly silence because he knew there was nothing he could do. He had no more fight left in him. His life had been nothing but fighting, and all he wanted to do was take care of his family, try not to cause any trouble and die in peace. Jim never looked at his dad quite the same after that, and when Jim left home at seventeen, he never went back. He refused to acknowledge the world really existed he'd grown up in where he was labeled, a nobody. His best friend Bobby had an uncle in Cleveland who said he could help them get jobs if they came, and when he left, it was the last time he ever stepped foot in Mississippi.

There were things his father had experienced growing up in the South that unfortunately Jim never knew about that his father thought him too young to be exposed to. Hell, some things were better left unspoken, and Jim never took that into consideration when judging his father for not being a man—for so harshly deciding to be so different from him. Funny, in all Jim's "accomplishments" he reveled in, he was never half the man his father was. His father had integrity, dignity, the fear of God and the love for family—traits Jim never quite picked up. But enough about Jim and the past for now.

Later that evening, Diane and Honey went to the airport to pick up June. They waited anxiously at the baggage claim as the passengers came down the escalator in groups.

"Why is it that the person you're waiting on always seems to be the last off the plane?" Honey said, standing on her tiptoes trying to spot June. "*Huuuh,* finally!" She ran toward June and grabbed her carry-on. "June Bug!"

The three of them hugged and headed for the baggage claim.

"I really need coffee," June blurted out in an exhausted voice. "Does this airport have a coffee bar? The coffee on the plane was horribly hideous."

"Oh, Lord." Honey rolled her eyes. "Really? Horribly hideous. Are you for real right now?" She laughed. "I forgot we are dealing with Miss Hollywood."

"Be quiet, Honey Dew." June laughed. "All I am saying is I need coffee."

"Ah, I hate it when you call me that."

"Yes, just like I hate it when you call me Dee," Diane scoffed.

They all laughed. It wasn't good to be home, but it was good to be with one another. These three shared a bond like no other, and they knew it. They had been through so much together, seen more than children should have to be exposed to and managed to halfway survive it all and not end up in the loony bin. Some broken places had healed, some wounds were still fresh as the day they happened, and the only love they trusted was the love they shared among the three of them.

"Let's get this child some coffee before she dies," Diane said.

"So, have you guys talked to Momma yet? Has she said anything about what happened?" June asked.

"No, not one word," Honey said.

"I tried when I first got here, but she said she wanted to wait until we were all here."

"*Hmmm.* Does that include Jim Jr.?" June asked.

"I don't think so. She made it seem like just us."

"Alrighty then."

"You how Momma is. She will talk when she is ready." Diane looked over at June to reassure her all was well.

I Don't Want to Remember

Their old house had four bedrooms, and each sister had her own room—until Jim Jr. came along, then Honey was moved into Diane's room. When they moved to a new house, which also had four bedrooms, which were just bigger, the sleeping arrangements stayed the same until June left, and Honey moved into June's old room. That was probably why Honey and Diane were just a little closer than Honey and June, but Diane and June were still thick as thieves because for the longest it was the two of them against not the world, but their father.

As they pulled into the driveway, June began to panic. "I don't think I wanna stay here. I wanna get a hotel. Take me to a hotel."

She began to physically shake as she flashed back to her childhood. Her mind immediately saw her father standing in the doorway calling out to her to come in.

It was a hot, sunny summer day, and she could not think of anything that she had done wrong, but yet there was something in his eyes that made her fearful.

"Yes, Daddy." She looked up from the tire swing she was lazing on in the backyard.

"Just get in here. Don't ask me any questions," he said.

She hopped off the swing and headed toward the door. She looked at him as she walked past, hanging her head. "Is everything okay, Daddy?"

He motioned her in. "It will be." He closed the door, looking out into the yard.

"It's okay, June. We're all going to be here. Besides, there's nothing bad that can happen anymore." Honey reached into the front passenger seat and rubbed June's shoulder.

Diane tried calming her down. "Momma is going to want all of us here. She is not going to want you to stay at a hotel, June. You already know that, so stop being dramatic and let's go." Diane turned the car off, gave June a no-nonsense yet reassuring look before getting out the car.

Honey jumped out from the back, grabbed June's bags and went in the door. June sat in the car as Diane leaned against the door talking to her through the window.

"I'll be right here until you're ready, but eventually you have to go in. I understand, and I'm not being mean, but this isn't about you. It's about Momma, and she needs us—all of us—and that includes you. I promise it will be okay. What are you paying that therapist all that money for if you can't even pull in the driveway? I'm confused."

Deep inside, June knew Diane was right. There was nothing there to harm her, but the memories that still jolted her from sleep seemed even more real looking at that old house. Josephine had kept it up, and though it was a beautiful house, there was a darkness that loomed over it. No matter what Josephine did to drown the darkness, it still lay on the surface, lurking, waiting to grab June, and no matter what anyone said, you could not tell her different. June sank down into the seat staring at the house for another twenty minutes before she slowly opened the door and exited the car. She stepped out, looked up at the sky and inhaled as if it was the last breath she would ever take.

"Ready?" Diane asked. June looked over at her exhaling and nodded in confirmation. They grabbed hands as they walked toward the door and entered the house.

June hardly ever came home. She would send for Josephine to visit her in California, but she always made excuses as to why she couldn't visit. Josephine didn't fully understand why, but it was an unspoken mental agreement that was never questioned. They made their way in, just as Josephine pulled a cake from the oven.

"Oh, now this, this is worth coming home for." Diane walked in and leaned over the cake, taking a big whiff.

"June Marie, why are you just standing there?" Josephine questioned.

"Sorry, Momma." She ran over to hug and kiss her after the cake was safely on the table.

"Look at this, my girls all here in one place. Never thought I would see this again." She stepped back filled with joy. "Well, had I known collapsing in a grocery store parking lot would bring you home together, I would have done it years ago." She chuckled. "Honey, pour the coffee. Diane, get the cake plates and a serving tray."

There was no need in the girls arguing they didn't need the formalities. This was who Josephine was. Things always had to be just so, and although Jim was gone, her perfection remained. If something went wrong, there would be no beating, no loud voice to berate her, but everything must be as it should, even when there were no consequences at hand. It was who she had become; it was who he had made her.

The girls sat in the living room drinking coffee, talking to Josephine before bed. There was really no need to catch up because they knew everything that was currently going on in one another's lives, but there was something about being face-to-face that gave them great comfort.

"Listen, girls, I feel fine. But I'm glad you all came so we can talk. Your mother is tired." She sighed and looked up at the ceiling. "The other day when I was walking out of the store, something came over me. I felt like I was ready to close the door on this side of life and open it on the other side."

She stood from her chair, pacing the floor in front of them, and all of a sudden, they felt like little girls again. Whenever Jim would act a fool or if Josephine knew he had been out drinking, she would bring the girls into the living room, sit them down and pace, explaining how they needed to stay in their rooms, but if they had to come out, not to upset Jim, not to ask him anything or make any conversation with him, and if he were to talk to them to agree with whatever he said because chances are he wouldn't remember the next day.

It was awful sometimes the three girls would all go get in June's bed because they felt safe when there were three, until one night Jim came home, and when he looked in Diane and Honey's room to make sure they were asleep, he began to rant and rave as to where they were. When he saw they were all together in June's bed, he blew up.

"I work every day and pay all this money for you to all sleep in one bed? Hell no." He snatched Honey out of the bed by and onto the floor by her hair, not even giving her the opportunity to simply stand up and walk down the hall and go to her room. Instead, while she was down, he grabbed both legs and drug her down the hall and threw her into her bed. She dared not kick and scream but allowed the tears to roll down the sides of her face silently.

As he came back for Diane, she was already on her way to the room. "Get down the hall," he screamed, "and don't let me catch you down here again."

He stood in June's doorway. "You know better than that. I better not ever come home and not be able to come in this room. You hear me?"

She sat there balled up, grasping her knees shaking as the tears burned him into a blur.

Josephine heard all the commotion and came down the hall. "Jim, come on here now and get some rest."

He just stood there looking at June. "See what you done started." He turned around and smacked Josephine. "Mind your business. Don't tell me what to do. You go get some rest if you want some."

He went down the stairs, and they heard the back door open and close. They waited and listened, and once they heard the car start and pull out the driveway, the three girls hopped up and ran to their mother.

No one ever knew what would set him off, but it was never good. These are the memories that came up just from a simple conversation over coffee in that house as Josephine continued with her explanation of her brief afterlife experience she was denied.

"Momma, what are you talking about? The doctor said you are perfectly healthy." Diane sat up.

"I didn't say I was sick, Diane. I said I'm tired—tired of living. There is nothing left for me on this side. You girls are gone and have your own lives, and I am happy about that, but I hardly see you, and Jim Jr., Lord knows I have tried all I can with him, but the only good thing from that boy is those babies. If it weren't for Charlene, I wouldn't see them as much as I do, I couldn't have asked for a better daughter-in-law. He doesn't come around that much anymore. He has his own life—Mr. Hotshot Real Estate Investor. Mabel's been gone now two years, and I feel like I'm just existing with no purpose. I keep asking the Lord why He still has me here. You girls could never understand because you have meaningful lives, and that's what I hoped for you. I don't expect you to be stopping your lives to amuse me."

"Mommy—" Honey began to cry—"I had no idea you felt like this. Why don't you sell the house and come live with me and Jared?"

"No, I am not going to be a burden on any of my children, so just hush your nonsense," she said adamantly.

"How could you be a burden?" Diane came over and stood next to her. "You are our mother. There's no us without you. You've taken care of us all our lives, and it's not like you need round-the-clock care or something. You aren't even old enough to think like this. What are you saying? You have plenty of life left to live. Women in their sixties work out at my gym. You could move to Atlanta with me. There's plenty to do there, and it's not the South you once knew. You could meet new people and—"

But Josephine stopped her as she walked over and stood in front of the fireplace with her back to the girls. She wept a silent cry on the inside. How could she make them understand? She'd lived her life; made peace with her decisions, good and bad; had a few regrets, but overall felt her purpose had been accomplished, raising her children and living up to the commitment and vows she had made before God to honor her marriage, no matter what, because that was considered the right thing to do back then. Eventually, God rescued her. Jim had been dead many, many years, and though she could have gotten remarried, she couldn't chance it, not that all men were bad, but how could she know. After all, she had done it right the first time, hadn't she? She'd prayed before she had gotten married, and she was a virgin—Jim was the only man she had ever been with. She did all that he had ever asked of her from cleaning his home to his drawers, and nothing was ever right—ever enough. Jim was never satisfied with the blessings God had given him. He would rather have the crumbs off the White man's table than eat the steak on his own.

Let's Talk About Josephine

J osephine was inexplicably beautiful. Men literally fought over her when she was coming up, but she chose Jim. He was handsome and smart. He could tell a story that would entrance and draw you in. Smooth talkers are what they were called back then, slick and sly, but Josephine in all her naiveté fell for the game. Fell hard, too. She loved Jim—until he sucked every last ounce of love for him from her. She had such dreams and hopes for their life together, but no matter how she tried, she was never enough, and he never let her forget it.

Josephine was born in South Carolina. She never knew who her father was. Though there were rumors Mr. William was her father, he nor her mother, Mae, ever said it. They lived in a small town, and everyone knew everyone, and they also knew Mr. William's wife did not play when it came to her man. In spite of this, everyone knew him and Mae had been creepin' around for years. Of course, they both denied anything was ever going on, but when she came up pregnant, there was no other man's baby it could have been, and as Josephine got older, she looked just like him.

Her mother was this beautiful, independent woman who loved her farm, her children, her sister, her men and her alcohol. Mae was strong and broke all the rules for women of her time— refusing to get married in the 1920s and 30s was crazy talk. But she refused to let a man own her was what she would say. Everything she had was hers. She owned it, and no one could take it from her. Josephine had a sister and a brother who knew their father, Mr. Ray. They were younger than Josephine, and though Mr. Ray loved Mae, she just wouldn't marry him. She loved men, but she didn't trust them, so no matter what Mr. Ray said, she was fine letting him move into her house and shack because if things went bad, she could always put him out and not the other way around.

That was their relationship too. He would make her mad, she would put him out, he'd be gone a few weeks, and she would take him back. That worked for them until one day it didn't. They had been foolin' around three years before she got pregnant with Josephine's brother, Bobby, and two years later, along came Gloria, her younger sister. Josephine was six when Bobby was born, and Mr. Ray always loved her and treated her like she was his, and she loved him back. He was a hard worker, and when he would get paid, he brought his money straight to Mae with no complaints. On Friday nights, after payday, Josephine would hear them laughing and drinking and making love real loud, things kids shouldn't hear but they did. Mr. Ray would ask again and again for Mae to marry him, but the answer never changed. She was solid in her no.

One Saturday morning, he got up and attempted to fix breakfast. He made the kids get up and get dressed up, and when Josephine had come in from the yard, he asked her again with the kids there to "make me the happiest man on the planet and be my wife," but the answer still remained no.

"Now damn it, Mae, I'm 'bout tired of this. I'm a man, and I love you, and I'm not gon' keep playing house with you and my children. I'm the joke of the town. People playin' me out to be some lovesick puppy who you the master of."

"Look, Ray, I done told you from the beginning I wasn't never gon' marry you or nobody else, so why ya keep askin' if you know I'mma tell you the same thing each time?"

"If you really loved me like you say you do, you would do the right thing and let me make an honest woman outta ya."

"What's that supposed to mean? I'm already an honest woman. I don't need a marriage paper to make me honest. Now I done heard enough of this. We just fine the way we is, Ray. Don't go messin' things up."

"No, Mae, you fine with how things is. I ain't. I want to be married. Plus, it's right in God's eyes. Marrying me is saying you commit to be with me forever like I wanna commit to be with you 'cause I love you."

"But we is committed," Mae pleaded with him. "I don't wanna be with nobody else. I'm here with you every day—day in and day out. I cook for you, clean up after you, wash yo' clothes, lay with you. We is committed as far as I'm concerned."

Ray looked long and hard at her before sitting down in the chair and putting his head in his hands. "Listen here, it's like this: Either you gon' marry me or you ain't. I want a wife."

"I'm sorry, Ray, but I just can't. Marriage ain't gonna change nothin'. We married in our hearts, that's where it counts, right? There is a whole bunch of people 'round here married on that piece of paper, but they ain't married in their hearts."

"I guess you would know 'bout that now, wouldn't you?" He stood and walked out. Mae couldn't believe he'd said that. She knew exactly what it meant, and he knew it would hurt her the way he was hurting. Yes, he was referring to Mr. William being Josephine's daddy even though he was married to someone else.

Things slowly started changing after that, and the Fridays that were once filled with laughter and lovemaking slowly turned to arguments and resentment. When Josephine was sixteen, one of those Friday nights, Mae and Ray were arguing, and Ray got his coat to leave.

When Mae questioned him, he turned and looked at her coldly. "I don't have to tell you nothing. You ain't my wife." Then he headed out the door, slamming it behind him. When one o'clock in the morning hit and Ray still wasn't home, Mae went looking for him.

She was talking to herself. "I can't believe I'm out here lookin' for a man." She chucked to her herself through her anger. "Yes, I guess I must love him." In the beginning, it wouldn't have bothered her if he didn't come home or if she wasn't made aware of his whereabouts, but this night it did.

She found herself at Eddie's bar looking through the window. She spotted Ray getting all snuggled up with Miss Lola. She could tell they had been there a while because they were good and drunk. She turned and went back home, aching from the inside out. She always said she would never allow a man to have emotional control over her, yet as she walked back home alone, she couldn't control her heart, which was being ripped to shreds.

Ray didn't come home that night, and when he came waltzing up the gravel drive that afternoon, all his things were on the front porch. There was nothing to be said or done. Josephine, Bobby and Gloria watched from the window as he kicked dirt and cussed and fussed, and the next day he moved his stuff into his daddy's barn and rented a room at Miss Lena's. Mae was never the same after that.

Josephine could never figure out what Mae had against marriage, and for as much as Mae hated marriage, Josephine believed in it. She often thought if she had been a little more like Mae, she may not have ended up in that mess of a marriage with Jim.

The story wasn't much different for Cora, Mae's sister—well, stepsister. They shared the same father but not the same mother. Cora's mother had died when Cora was three, and when Cora's father met Mae's mother, Winnie, they got married. They were not a poor black southern family. They definitely were not well-to-do, but her stepfather owned land, and they had a beautiful farm and a comfortable house. It was just Cora and Mae, and they were sisters by all accounts.

Now, it was no secret that Cora had been involved with Robert Hines when they were teenagers, He claimed he loved her, they were going to have a bunch of kids and live happily ever after. He and Cora were not having sex because she wanted to wait, and Robert Hines respected that, just not enough to wait too. When he got Maxine pregnant, her daddy said he was going to marry her, and he did. Cora never got over that. She rushed and married the first thing that asked in an attempt to cover her pain and get back at Robert, but that didn't turn out so well. One day she woke up, and he was gone.

Shortly thereafter, she realized she was pregnant with little Audrey. It was hard trying to work and take care of a baby, and even with their mother and Mae's help, it was still hard. She was lonely, and old Robert Hines was the only way she knew to cheer herself up. Even after Cora met Jackson, she still needed a little cheering up sometimes, and well, one of those times brought about little Paulene.

There were no DNA tests back then. Your daddy was whoever your momma said it was, and that was that, No matter how much speculation, it would be just that, speculation. Cora was a good mother, but she battled her own demons and alcohol, which seemed to run in the family.

Robert Hines was the way she dealt with them, but he was also at the root of them. Don't understand wrong. Cora took her girls to church every Sunday along with Mae's children, and even though she couldn't always uphold the values that were being taught, she hoped her girls could. She wanted to be better, but she just didn't have it in her.

Both Cora and Mae grew mean and a little bitter but disguised it with men and liquor, dying much sooner than they should have. Mae never gave Ray a chance to explain about that night in the bar, and when Josephine was nineteen, Ray moved to Ohio for a job opportunity, and Josephine went with him. She had big dreams but never having finished high school, work options were very limited for

her. She ended up becoming a cocktail waitress, which was how she
met Jim Holloway

When They Met

Many nights after getting off the second shift, Jim and his best friend, Bobby, whose uncle got them their jobs in Cleveland, would frequent a lounge to blow off steam, have a few drinks and relax before they went home to sleep so they could rise and do it all again the next day. It had become their way of life, and though it was a much different way, it wasn't exactly the life Jim had dreamed of, but it was much better than the life he had left in Mississippi. In Cleveland, a man could be a man. He could make a decent wage, wear fine clothes and even drive a nice car, as long as he stayed on his side of town.

This was always Jim's problem. He always wanted what was off limits to him. He felt like he was a man as any other man, so how come another man got to decide what was right for him because of his skin color? It just wasn't right.

Jim saw Josephine, and she was the most beautiful Black woman he had ever laid eyes on—looked like she could have been right off the movie screen. She came over to him and Bobby, holding her small serving tray with a flared skirt too short to bend over without exposing all her goods.

"What can I get for you gentlemen?" Her smile let off rays of sun as she waited for their response. This was the chance encounter that changed her life.

Because of her beauty, Josephine made tips that others were often jealous of, which allowed her to buy nice dresses and shoes—

things other women her age only dreamed of. Every time she and Jim went out, they were usually one of if not the most well-dressed, attractive couples no matter where they went. Jim liked this. He felt like a million bucks knowing he had the woman most men in the room wanted but couldn't have. He boasted his chest and showed off his trophy.

Things seemed to go well for them. Jim was funny but serious about work and getting ahead in life. They would hold hands and talk for hours. He would share his dreams, and she would support them, no matter how farfetched they were. When she looked into his eyes, she saw strength and protection, and with all his big talk, she saw security. If anyone could accomplish what they set out to do, it was Jim. She encouraged him and believed in him, and deep down, she knew if she stuck it out, his success would be her success.

Bobby had a soft spot in his heart for Josephine from the day they both met her, but it was clear she was smitten with Jim's smooth operating sell of himself. Bobby turned out to be a much better man, but as they say hindsight is always 20/20.

Though times started out good for Jim and Josephine, life and bitter demons weighed heavy on Jim, and eventually the bad times got really bad, and they overshadowed and far outweighed the good ones, no matter how good. Jim tried to love Josephine, but he was so busy hating her for not being what he could not have and in turn began to hate himself. He didn't know why he wanted to be accepted by Whites so bad. He wanted to prove he was just as good as them and deserved everything they had and more.

Jim worked his way up at the plant, which was a hard thing to do during the sixties, but some companies in Cleveland believed in fair pay and equal opportunity before it was common practice, and fortunately for him, he was well liked. In spite of how he turned out, God had given Jim favor with man. Maybe it was because of the heartbreak he witnessed and lived growing up in the racist Mississippi world. Possibly it was dealing with the blatant disregard for his life based solely on his skin color. Whatever the case, people liked him. He had a way with words and charm that stretched far as the eye could see.

One man, Paul, became especially close to Jim and Josephine. He was a businessman and had done well with investing. He and Jim had met at the bank when Jim was trying to see about getting a loan to open a small corner store. Jim was not surprised he was denied, but he wanted to try. Paul had overheard him talking to the loan officer and quite frankly was impressed by how prepare and determined he appeared to be. He waited around outside for Jim to come out and introduced himself.

"Hi." Paul stuck his hand out for Jim to shake it. "I didn't catch your name inside. I'm Paul Barker."

Jim hesitantly grabbed his hand with a firm grip and shook. "Jim. It's Jim Holloway."

"I couldn't help but overhear your proposal for your store, and I would like to sit down and talk to you more about it. I may be able to help."

"Yes. How do you figure that?"

Do you have time to meet me at my office and discuss some ideas I'd like to share with you?"

Jim wasn't sure if the guy was sincere, playing a joke on him or if it was a setup, but he went, and this was the beginning of a true friendship. Jim had never been friends with a White man before—he had been acquainted with coworkers, but never friends. Paul showed Jim a different side of life, and the more Jim saw, the more Jim wanted.

Jim had saved money over the years—he was good at saving—but he still needed a loan if he was going to open a small neighborhood store. Now Paul didn't loan him the money. He invested in the store, and they became partners. Paul was an honest man who saw an opportunity to help someone else out while helping himself as well. Jim eventually gave Paul money to invest for him because Paul understood the market and investing, and over time, Jim learned to trust him. A lot of the money Jim made was thanks to Paul. In some respects, it was almost as if he wanted to be him.

Jim introduced Josephine to Laura, Paul's wife. He wanted very much for her to be like Laura. He would take her shopping and buy her clothes similar to Laura's, and he wanted her to try and style her hair like Laura's, even act like her. Josephine knew what Jim was doing but she knew she was never going to be Laura, nor was she meant to be. Josephine knew in her heart this was unfortunate for her because what Jim wanted, he was determined to have, at all cost. If she could have just miraculously turned into Laura, her problems would have all been solved, but since she couldn't, their friendship with the Barkers only intensified Jim's rage toward Josephine.

In Steps Jane

E ventually, the attempt to transform Josephine was abandoned once Jane entered the picture. Blonde, blue-eyed perfection. Jane was Paul's new assistant, and Jim was drawn to her strikingly beautiful appearance. She was completely wooed by his charm and good looks, and there was nothing sweeter to Jim than plucking fruit from the forbidden tree of the times. The harmless flirting quickly turned into secret rendezvous that were exciting, mainly because they were so forbidden. Paul would definitely not have approved of this, not because Jane was White, but he really liked Josephine. He just had no idea Jim did not. So, their secret stayed just that, a secret, Jim didn't even want her telling her friends because he didn't trust them not to tell others, and though she told him she would never tell, of course she did.

Jane would brag to her girlfriends about that Black god who was the complete opposite of what she had been taught her whole life about Black men. There were very few places they could go together in Cleveland publicly at that time, and even the few places they could, they were given dirty and strange looks. Eventually, most of their time was spent at her apartment or being snuck in and out of hotels, but Jane fell hard for him. She described their lovemaking in detail to her two closest friends and watched their faces in disbelief. He made love to her in a way that would bring any woman to her knees, and though Josephine stroked his ego, nothing stroked it like tasting that fruit and having that fruit long for you and desire you and do anything for you.

The longer he was with Jane, the more he resented Josephine for only being able to be what God had made her, a beautiful Black woman. But again, we'll talk about Jane more a little later.

Meet Jim Jr.

T here would be no discussion of Josephine living with any of the girls. It would not be an option, no matter how logical it was or how much each of them loved her.

"Okay, girls, that's enough for tonight." She spoke, still not facing them, "I will see everyone in the morning."

The girls continued to sit, wanting to discuss the topic further.

"I said I will see everyone in the morning."

And they knew that meant exit the room, and so they did. They filed one by one out of the living room. Diane began to pick up the plates on her way out.

"Leave it, Diane. I will get it," Josephine said.

"I don't mind, Momma. I will clean up. You go ahead and rest."

"I said leave it and go on ahead upstairs." Diane quickly set the plate in her hand onto the serving tray and headed up the stairs joining June and Honey who were both in June's room.

"And do not, I repeat do not, discuss this any further when you get up those stairs," Josephine called out from the living room.

She lingered in front of the fireplace a bit, pondering life and its pain-filled purpose before clearing the plates away and cleaning the kitchen.

No sooner than Josephine had told them not to talk about the situation, the girls all sat on June's bed trying to make sense of what was happening, but they couldn't. They wanted to fix it for their mother, but they couldn't. These were scars that had healed with infection under them. Some scars of life never go away. Even with God's help, a choice has to be made to take power over the scars and not let the scars have the power. Sometimes the scars keep us from becoming who we were intended to be.

"What are we going to do?" Honey looked fretful. "She's scaring me. Do you think she would kill herself? She sounds suicidal. I mean, I can't imagine Momma would do something like that, but I don't like how she was talking—you know, the things she was saying. It's crazy, right?"

The more she thought and talked, the more frantic Honey became. "I don't like this." She stood and began pacing. "I don't like this not one bit."

Her voice became shaky, and her stomach churned in tiny knots. Diane stood and put her arm around Honey to try and comfort her, saying there was nothing they could do that night and they should take Momma's advice, go to bed and see one another in the morning. They all believed this was quite logical advice, yet no one moved, and an hour later, there they sat, as confused and helpless as when they first entered the room.

"Do you think we should just ask her?" Diane asked, nearly rubbing a stuffed bunny from June's chair to the point of hairlessness.

"Ask her what?" June asked.

"You know, if she is thinking about you know, ending it," Diane replied.

"Stop it. We're Black. She is not hardly about to kill herself. We have endured a lot as a people. I highly doubt feeling tired is what's going to push her over the edge. Don't be stupid. Besides, if she didn't put herself out of her misery as many obstacles as she has faced in life, do you really think loneliness will be the deal breaker? I mean be for real, this is our mother we're talking about. She's a survivor. She was married to Daddy of all people. If that wasn't reason enough to take her out, I doubt anything else will," June said sternly.

June was right, wasn't she? Josephine was strong and had been the rock of their existence. There is no way she would do that, right? Especially not with all of us here, or maybe this would be the perfect time to do it, because all of us are here. She would not do it the first night though, Diane thought. She would want to spend as much time with us as possible before going to the other side.

Diane jumped up. "Okay, I'm going to bed. I thought about it, and she definitely is not going to kill herself tonight. She wouldn't do that to us the first night we're home. She knows it would be too traumatic for us to handle, especially knowing how much we hate coming here. If anything, it would be the last night, so let's deal with this after we've rested and can all think straight."

And as simple as that, Diane's word was the last word as it often was, and everyone went to bed.

The next morning, Diane called Jim Jr., who had officially renamed himself William. As much as he loved and respected Jim, he said William was more dignified than Jim. On occasion, he had said the name Jim rang slavery or share cropper in his opinion, and he, like his father, wanted more out of life. When he got into real estate, he simply changed it, just like that. No one in their family honored that change, but outside of the Holloway home, he was officially William Holloway, and he had the business card to prove it.

Diane had reluctantly called him to come to the house because she knew it was what Josephine wanted. Josephine loved her son because he came from her, but he was truly his father's child, and though she was not excited to see him, she always enjoyed seeing the children and Charlene, his wife. They all sat around the table eating the huge brunch Josephine had prepared.

It was sickening watching Charlene waiting on Jim Jr. hand and foot, not to mention her having to do everything for the children too. But these sisters had no idea how bad it was until Charlene had an opinion about their son William, and football, which conflicted with Jim's, and he grabbed Charlene by the arm and told her that was enough.

As she went to say, "But I…"

He grabbed her face and said, "I said that's enough."

This pissed the girls off, but especially Diane. "What the hell is wrong with you? Get your hands off her. Are you crazy?"

She stood, and Jim Jr. did not back down. "This is my wife. Mind your damn business."

Diane looked over at Charlene. "Does he hit you?"

He interrupted. "I said mind your business, Diane."

He looked over at Charlene with a threatening look to ensure she would be too intimidated to answer. No words were necessary— her silence said it all.

"This is ridiculous. I cannot believe you're going to sit there and take that. No one can fight for you until you're willing to fight for yourself." Diane shook her head, sat down, and asked for another waffle. "Wow, Jim Jr., I knew you were an asshole. I just didn't know how much of one you were until this very minute. I cannot even sit in here and watch this." She grabbed her plate with her waffle, attempting to head into the kitchen.

"My name is William!"

Charlene wasn't weak, but she liked the lifestyle Jim Jr. afforded her. He got her straight from the projects, and though she was in community college when she met him, she was dealing with her reality of being a poor Black girl living with a single mother and four siblings. She wanted a way out, and Jim Jr. gave her that. He wined and dined her, and he loved her the best way he could, but he learned a dysfunctional love that his mother could not correct, no matter how hard she tried. Maybe had she left Jim, Jim Jr. would have seen women, money and power a little differently, but the reality was she didn't leave, she stayed and he was who he was. Jim Jr. did not beat Charlene as Jim did Josephine, but he spoke harshly, and he would slap her or grab her here and there, but she accepted this for the house she lived in, the car she drove, the clothes she wore and for her children to never know what it was like to be hungry or embarrassed by the clothes they wore to school.

She finally looked up. "It's fine, Diane. Don't leave. There's nothing to worry about."

"Yeah, Diane. It's fine." Jim Jr. chuckled and shook his head.

But in Diane's opinion, this was not fine. What was fine about this? It wasn't fine when it was done to Josephine, and it wasn't fine now. What alternate universe were they living in? She looked hard and long at Jim Jr. "I can't stand to look at you. Be careful you don't end up like your father since you wanna be him so bad." Honey and June looked at Diane, stunned.

"Diane," Honey exclaimed. But Diane looked cold and hard at Jim Jr. as if it wasn't karma but more of a warning. She burned a hole through him as she exited the room. The girls had not seen that much hate spewing from Diane since Jim was alive, and they knew it all too well.

When Josephine got pregnant with Jim Jr., it was the same story as Honey—same beating, different year. The only difference was this time Jim got himself a son out of the deal, and he could not have been more proud. He was almost nice for a while, keyword being *almost*. Jim could only be as nice as someone as horrible as he was could be.

He beamed with pride when the doctor came out and told him it was a boy.

"Little Jim," he said. "I got myself a little me." He gazed at Jim Jr. "You gonna be somebody. You remember that. You meant to be somebody just like I was meant to be somebody, and don't you let the world and nobody in it tell you no different." He cradled him.

The doctor looked over at Jim. "Yes, Mr. Holloway, everybody knows you. There's nothing like having a son to carry on your legacy. It's a good one from what I can tell—a true namesake."

He chuckled. "If I could, all three of my boys would be named after me."

Jim was still beaming with pride. "You're right, Doc. I've done a fine job with the cards I was dealt. He's lucky to have a man like me for a father, not like my daddy. I am nothing like my daddy." He stood slapping his chest with one fist. "Jim Jr. it is!"

When they first brought Jim Jr. home, Jim spent more time at home than he had in years—even put his little side girlfriend Jane on the backburner for a while, but that was short lived. Jane wasn't having that for too long, new baby or not. She would call the house and hang up if Jim didn't answer. If she did it too many times in one day, he knew that was his cue she was getting mad and he needed to go make things right for her. As much as he hated Josephine, he loved Jane that much more. Many of the things he did for Jane as a girlfriend, he did not even do for Jane as his wife. He never wanted her to be upset and never wanted to see her cry. Whenever Jane even looked as if she had a tear in her eye, Jim gave into whatever she would request—money, clothes, a car, leaving his family to spend time with her during holidays and especially Sunday dinner. She knew Sunday was family day after church, but eventually it became family day at her house not his own. He even took Jim Jr. with him sometimes.

Even though in reality Jim made it clear there was no competition for his affection, Josephine was still his wife, and Jane wanted that. She pushed her way in to every area of Jim's life— eventually there were almost no boundaries.

Over the years, Jim Jr. could do no wrong, Jim made Josephine wait on him hand and foot—the golden child is what Diane and June often called him. When Jim Jr. was smaller, he loved Josephine, after all he was home with her all day, and she truly did dote over him. He would look up at her with the biggest grins and laugh so heartily when they would play, but as the years went by, he began to see her through the eyes of Jim. It seemed as if he forgot she had always been there for him, feeding, bathing, playing and everything else a mother does. As Jim Jr. got older, he watched Jim who seemed to have grown even more bitter and meaner toward his mother. She could never do anything right. He looked for reasons to hit her or yell at her, and this often took place in front of the children, and eventually Jim Jr. began to slowly see Josephine through Jim's eyes and began to treat her similarly. He never raised his hand to her but disregarded things she would say or threatened to tell Jim if she did not give him his way. It was sad to see Jim's blood pumping through their son's veins turning his heart cold.

Honey was the only one who sometimes felt sorry for him, oftentimes wondering what chance he ever had with Jim as a role model, but believing at some point everyone has to take responsibility for their actions, for their rights and wrongs. Jim never did, so maybe Jim Jr. never would either. Jim's life was cut short but not before having the opportunity to leave a trail of emotional destruction along the way for everyone he came in contact with before his untimely death.

Death Was Good

J im was murdered when the kids were teenagers, all except June. She was twenty, and his murder was never solved. During the mid-1970s, things were changing a lot for Blacks, but not enough that the city was going to spend a whole lot of tax dollars to solve the mystery of a Black man who looked as if he were in the wrong place at the right time. Josephine was heartbroken. Regardless of what he had put her through, she still felt the loss. She loved the man she met so many years ago and secretly held on to the hope he would return. However, relief filled her, and the foreign space of familiar fear had fled, replacing it with the rising fear of the unknown. They would be okay financially as long as she worked a little. The life insurance was not enormous by any means, but it was enough. Paul offered to buy her out of the store if she did not want to have the responsibility.

She would find that Jim had done alright for himself, even better than she thought. Josephine had completely forgotten what it was like not to walk on eggshells every day of her life, but she knew it was going to be difficult to be free. This new freedom caused her to never push hard for the police to investigate the inconsistencies that loomed over his death. She knew something wasn't right. But she just figured, this was God's way of making some of her pain stop. She hated Jim had to lose his life for her to gain hers, but she had given up so much of it already.

Who was she? There was a small remnant of the young fiery girl that had left South Carolina so many years ago, with eyes wide open and a heart full of passion for life. She did not know how to be without Jim telling her who he needed her to be, but hopefully she would slowly find herself.

The night Jim was killed, Josephine was just relieved he didn't come home. She had no idea why he wasn't there, but when she woke up the next morning and he still wasn't there, she felt something wasn't right. When he would stay out late, he would usually come home drunk and either want to manhandle her sexually or fight her. Both were equally as painful, so she would never be able to fall asleep and rest well because she was always waiting, preparing for him to come in, but not this night. This night, she finally fell off to sleep, and she slept until the sun came up. When she realized it was morning and saw Jim's side of the bed was untouched, she checked the couch, no Jim. She went out to see if maybe he had fallen asleep in his car. Not only was there no Jim, there was no car. Jim did his thing, but he was usually home long before the sun came up.

By nine a.m., she was concerned. She picked up the phone and called Bobby. They often hit the bars together. His wife, Betty, answered. She apologized for calling so early but asked Betty to ask Bobby if he had heard from Jim, but he hadn't. After calling the police and being told nothing could be done at that point, she began to panic. She knew in her heart something had happened—this wasn't like him. She swallowed her pride, picked up the phone and called Jane.

"Hello." A cheery, refreshingly angelic voice picked up on the other end.

Josephine cleared her throat, took a deep breath and swallowed hard. "Jane, this is Josephine…. Hello. Are you there?" Josephine questioned.

There was a pause and a slight panic in Jane's voice. She knew exactly who Josephine was, but she acted as if she was unsure and clueless. As bold as she was in her relationship with Jim when she heard Josephine on the other end, she was not ready to be confronted by her truth. Whatever truth that may be.

"I'm sorry, Josephine who?"

"Please, let's not do this." Josephine was irritated.

"Why are you calling me? Does Jim know you are calling me?" she asked nervously.

"Look, Jane, I'm not calling you to question your relationship with Jim. I could care less."

Josephine cared, but she knew there was nothing she could do about it. She didn't want to accept that Jim was an adulterer. It's not how she had pictured her life going, but she accepted Jim, and it was part of who he was.

"I need to know if you've heard from him. He seems to be missing, and I thought you might know where he was."

"Why no, I have not."

"Now, Jane, you know you don't have any reason to lie if you have." Josephine did not believe her.

"No, no, I really haven't seen or heard from him."

"Hmmm. Okay." Josephine didn't say goodbye, simply placed the receiver onto the phone base. She stood in the kitchen and began to pray. She hoped he was alright.

When the girls came down, there was no breakfast that morning. No smell of biscuits permeating the house, and no crisp bacon waiting to be preyed upon by the kids. Diane strolled down the stairs about ten, wondering exactly where the food was, but there was none.

"Good morning, Momma. No breakfast today?" she joked. "Would you like me to throw something together?"

"No, Diane, I can do it. Your father isn't home."

"So." Diane shrugged.

"No, I mean, he didn't come home last night, and he's still not here. I'm a bit worried."

"Why? You know Daddy. He'll come strolling in any minute wreaking all kinds of havoc, especially if there is no food prepared."

"Diane, no, I think there's something wrong. This isn't like Jim. You know what I mean, it's just not. Something must have happened—something has to be wrong."

Diane and Josephine began to cook. Diane was doing most of the cooking while Josephine was doing all of the worrying. Soon, Honey came in and began squeezing the oranges for the juice while there was still no sign of June. Eventually, they were all sitting around the kitchen table eating and making their best attempt to be normal, but Jim's chair being empty was a clear indication all was not well. The girls were honestly relieved, but they were only concerned for Josephine who seemed to be unraveling.

Jim and Josephine always went to the grocery store Saturdays, and usually the earlier the better. This was something he had done from the beginning of their marriage, and they continued, just no longer with children in tow. Even if Jim had been out philandering, he would surely be home by now. She even asked Jim Jr. if he knew where Jim might be. It was no secret he knew many of Jim's secrets, including his women.

"How would I know where he is? I'm here with you. I'm not with him," he said sarcastically.

The girls attempted to comfort her and tell her not to worry, that he was probably just out being Jim. No matter what they said, she knew different.

"Momma, really, I'm sure everything is fine. You know how Daddy is. He probably drank too much and didn't mean to spend the night wherever he is and now doesn't want to come home and face us." Honey rubbed her shoulder.

"Face us like what? You mean maybe he is too tired to fight. And we all know he is never too tired for that. Since when did Daddy care about what any of us thought?" June blurted out. "I wouldn't care if he never came back."

"Hush. There will be no such talk in this house." Josephine was becoming frustrated. She got up and called Mabel who immediately came over. She was there for support, but she shared the same sentiment as June—goodbye and good riddance to bad rubbish, and Jim definitely fit that bill.

At 5:23 p.m. that very day, the doorbell rang. Josephine, Bobby, Betty and Mable were sitting in the kitchen drinking coffee and worrying. Diane went to the door. It was two police officers. There was a huge pit in the bottom of her stomach when she saw them standing there.

"Who is it?" Josephine called from the kitchen.

"Is Mrs. Holloway home?" one of the officers asked.

"*Ummm,* yes." She hesitated. "What is this regarding?"

"We need to speak with her immediately."

"One second. I'll get her."

Diane looked over at Honey sitting on the couch and glanced up at June who was standing on the stairs as she made her way to the kitchen. "*Ummm,* Momma, *ummm…*"

"What is it, Diane? Spit it out."

"The police are at the door."

Josephine sat there. "I knew it. I knew something wasn't right." She stood to take the short walk from the kitchen to the front door, which seemed like an eternity. She saw the look on the officers' faces, and she knew. She knew they had to break some bad news to her. They had the solemn-officer-giving-bad-news face, both of them. She finally reached the door and opened it, allowing the officers to step in out of the July heat.

"*Ummm,* good evening, Mrs. Holloway." The taller officer looked at her. "I am so sorry to inform you we found your husband, Jim Holloway. Unfortunately, he appears to have been murdered."

"He what?" Josephine looked confused.

"I am very sorry, Mrs. Holloway, but he appears to have been murdered. Can you think of anyone who may have wanted to harm him?"

They waited but she was unable to speak.

When the officers arrived on the scene, Jim was found slumped over onto the car steering wheel. It appeared he had been stabbed twice. There was a blood trail coming from the side of the building leading to his car. The detectives figured he managed to get the car door open and get in, but his keys were found on the driver's side floor mat. They thought maybe he was going to attempt to drive to the hospital or possibly even home, not realizing the extent of his injuries. He bled out before even starting the car. Not sure why he didn't just try to make it back to the main road where someone may have seen him.

"His car was parked on Clawson Street, but the establishment he was parked next to is not open after hours. Do you know what he may have been doing there or where he may have actually been?"

"Quite honestly, officers, I don't know much about Jim's night life." She seemed dazed and began to reach out as she suddenly hit the floor.

"Momma," Honey screamed.

"Give her some air," one of the officers said.

"Momma," Honey cried out again.

The officer kneeled, took her pulse and felt her head "She fainted. Grab a cold towel and some water."

Mabel ran and got water, and Betty ran and got a cold towel.

"Mrs. Holloway?" The officer shook her gently and continued calling her name.

"Has she eaten anything today?" the other officer asked. She began to slowly open her eyes. "Here she comes. Are you okay, Mrs. Holloway?"

"I feel a little woozy." She attempted to sit up.

"No, don't try and sit up, just lay there for a minute and get your bearings," the officer said. "Give yourself a minute."

Ten minutes later, they were able to help her up to the couch. "I know this isn't easy, but do you think you are okay to answer a few questions for us?"

"No, no. Actually, I am not okay. You just informed me my husband is dead." She just sat there staring out into space. "This cannot be happening. Who would do this to him? Everyone loves Jim. He doesn't have any enemies. This just doesn't make sense. It doesn't make sense." She stood but sat right back down. "This is just unreal."

"Mrs. Holloway, I understand this has to be hard, but is there anything you can think of that may be able to help us find out who may have done this to your husband?"

"Betty—I mean, Bobby—do you know where he was last night?"

"No, Josephine, I wish I did. I saw him at work yesterday, and we stopped and had a drink, but he left the same time I did, and that was about six-thirty." Bobby struggled to understand what could have happened between then and now. Jim was his best friend. They had known each other their whole lives.

Josephine looked over at Jim Jr. "Do you know anything that can help them find out who did this to your father. Anything?" she pleaded.

Jim Jr. stood there dumbfounded. "N–No," he stuttered. "No, I wish I did." It was as if the wind was knocked from him. He was Jim's sidekick. He stood there lost for words and void of expression.

"You'll need to go down to the morgue and identify the body. I'm going to leave my card. If there's anything that comes to you, please give me a call," the tall officer said. He then motioned to speak with Bobby outside.

Both officers turned to leave, stating they were sorry for the family's loss. Josephine continued to sit there. She leaned back onto the couch, listening to the officers' shoes hit each step as they departed the porch. She felt the reality and the gravity of the situation with each step. The pound of each shoe sole kicked at her heart. Though she wanted to lay there, she knew she had to get up, if not for her, for the kids. What was she going to do now? Dysfunction was who she had become and all she knew to be. Long gone was the bright-eyed, ambitious girl who had come with a heart full of hope, only to trade it for a life full of woes.

The next few days were rough to say the least. The girls were mixed up. They were glad Jim was gone, but they knew it wasn't right to feel that way, but they did. They were sad only because their mother was sad. She really did love Jim in all his flaws. That was that real unconditional love most people don't have—that ole school Black love. That stand-by-your-man-and-make-excuses-for-him love. That love that was willing to be the sacrificial lamb for what Black men had experienced and would continue to experience for years to come. Josephine tried to understand his experiences and be there for him, but no one would ever understand Jim and what made him tick.

Many men had suffered racial prejudice and weren't like Jim, but unfortunately, there were many others that were just like him, some even worse. The people who loved Josephine believed she took that unconditional love a little too far. Her friend Mabel told her she should have been gone years ago. Although it wasn't that simple back then, once she started popping out all those babies, what would she do? How would she take care of them? Many were just happy their men stuck around after all the babies were born. Besides, how would they have lived if she had chosen to leave? But that was neither here nor there now. The fact was Jim was gone, and she had stuck it out for better or worse.

Jim Jr. took it pretty hard, he and Jim were so close, and in his eyes, Jim did no wrong, even when he did things Jim Jr. knew were wrong. Jim Jr. was trained by his father. He was just being a man living the best he could with the hand he had been dealt. He never saw how wrong it was the way Jim treated Josephine, He really believed if she did better, then Jim wouldn't be so hard on her, but no matter how perfect she attempted to be, Jim still found fault with her. When a boy witnesses the abuses and rage Jim displayed in their home, he is going to do one of two things: emulate and aspire to be like his father, or he will despise the actions of the man and vow to be nothing like him. Jim Jr. chose the latter.

Jim's mother, Ruth, as well as some of his siblings came up to lay him to rest, but none of them knew Jim—not the Jim they probably remembered. He had become a very different man. They had no idea how he treated Josephine, and his mother had only met her once early in the marriage when Josephine first had June. She caught the train up with such excitement to see this grandbaby. After that, anytime his mother made an effort to visit, Jim always came up with an excuse as to why she couldn't, and eventually she stopped asking.

Jim's sister, Joy, told the girls stories of how much their parents loved each other, how they did the best they could and that they loved Jim and all his siblings so much. But Jim, Jim was different. He had no respect for his parents after that day at the store. It changed him. He seemed to resent being Black because Blacks had it so hard.

Joy and Sam were the two siblings above Jim and the closest in age.

"Yo' daddy was something else." Sam leaned back in the chair laughing. "There was nothing he set his mind to that he wasn't gonna do, you can best believe that. When he left, I almost came with him, but I was a little too nervous, and my life seemed to be coming along pretty good, so why go takin' a chance and messin' it up, ya know? But not Jim. He was willing to risk it all, but I guess it paid off. Look at this beautiful house and beautiful family. I just hate it took him passing away for us to get to meet you all. We missed so much of ya lives."

The family went and joined Josephine and Jim Jr. as they sat at the dining room table putting the obituary together. After all the negativity experienced at Jim's hands, Josephine gave him the utmost respect with the words expressed on each page. No one would know him as anything other than the man he displayed outside their home. The charismatic, handsome, loving and kind man everyone else saw. Jim Jr. had pictures the girls and Josephine had never seen from Jim's childhood. There weren't many, but it allowed them to see what he looked like as a child and where he grew up. Jim had given those pictures to Jim Jr when he was thirteen along with a watch.

Ruth looked down on the table and saw the pictures William and Josephine had out on the table

"Wow. This brings back memories. Look at cha brother in those shorts and that cap, lookin' like somebody just gave him a million dollars with that grin." Her eyes began to tear up. "He could charm a snake if he had to. I just can't imagine anyone wanting to kill my baby."

"No?" Diane mumbled.

"What's that, Diane baby?" Ruth looked over at her, confused.

"Nothing." She got up and left the room.

"Oh, wait. What is this? Why do you guys have a picture of Anna out here?" Joy blurted.

"Who?" Josephine asked.

"Anna." Joy picked up the picture.

"Now, that's yesterday's news. Let's not go diggin' that up." Ruth looked over at Joy.

"I'm not diggin' up nothin'. It's right here in front of me."

"So, who is she?" Honey questioned.

"Honey darling, that was a long time ago—almost another life—and that's where we gon' leave it," Ruth said gently.

"Where did it come from though?" Joy asked.

"It was in a box that Jim had given to Jim Jr. along with some other pictures and various things," Josephine offered.

Sam took that as his cue to give up a little insight, "She was a long time ago, that Anna Elizabeth Jackson. She lived down the road from us when we were growing up, and yo' daddy had a thing for her, and she had one for him. You know back then, there wasn't a whole lot to do, so Anna and Jim spent a lot of time at the lake talking about their big dreams for the future. Yo' daddy would tell me how they were going to get out of their small town and move to a big city and be everything society told them they would never be."

"Well, what's the big deal?" Honey questioned again. "Who is she? I wanna know."

"It's not appropriate, Honey," Ruth said, looking over at Josephine.

"It's okay, Ruth. Whatever it is, it doesn't really matter at this point."

This was Joy's ticket to talk as she loved to do, so she began, "Anna was your daddy's first love, but a bigger life called him, and he had to decide between love and dreams. Jim wanted Anna to come to Ohio with him, but her father would hear of no such thing. She was going to stay there in Mississippi and finish school, maybe even get the opportunity to go away to college, and he didn't want Jim filling her head with dreams of nonsense and disrupting her education—at least that's what she told me. There was no way Jim was going to be able to take her with him when he first left, and he promised the night before he left he would come back for her when she finished high school, but he never did."

Anna's Role in Jim Becoming

T he night before Jim left for Cleveland, he and Anna lay at the
lake as they normally did.

"One day, Anna, I'mma get you outta here, and I'mma give
you everything you want." Jim looked up into the night sky next to
Anna on the blanket they often brought to the lake with them.

"*Ummm-hmmm,* and how you gonna do that, Mr. Holloway?"
she said in a dreamy, hopeful voice, smiling in the night as the moon
danced across her golden-brown skin.

"We gonna start in Cleveland but who knows, Chicago,
maybe even New York, and I'm gonna get a good job and make a lot
of money and take care of you, and won't nobody be able to hurt you.
I'm gonna buy you fancy dresses and take you to fine restaurants like
the White folk."

"*Aww,* Jim, I don't need none of that stuff. As long as we
together, that's all I need to make me happy."

"Lizzie—" that's what Jim called her— "I'm gonna be
somebody one day, you gonna see, and you gonna be so happy."

"Jim, honestly, I'm happy now. I don't need much, and I'll
follow you wherever you go. I love you, Jim Holloway."

He rolled over, leaning on his elbow, looking at her. "I love
you too."

The two loved one another as much as two teenagers could,
and for them, the love was real. It was strong, and they loved hard.
The common struggles of growing up in Mississippi drove them to

cleave to one another tightly. They understood one another. As they lay there, they hoped the night would never end. They both knew tomorrow would come too soon and the reality of separation was almost too much to bare.

"Lizzie, you gon' let me tonight before I leave?"

"Jim, you know I can't do that. We ain't married."

"But I'm coming back for you soon as I can afford to make a life for us. You know I'm gon' marry you. Who else gonna have me?" He chuckled, "Ain't nobody more right for two people besides us." He kissed her hard and long and began undressing her.

"Wait." She protested, but the waits became fainter and fainter, and before long, they were making love on the same blanket that had not known passion before. Anna was torn with the decision. She was glad she had pleased Jim before he was leaving, and she hoped it showed how much she loved him and believed in him.

"I promise you, I won't let you down, Lizzie, and when I come back for you, you better be ready." He held her as they talked until the sun came up, and though she knew she would be in trouble when she got home, she didn't care. She was where she needed to be.

That afternoon, everyone gathered around saying their goodbyes to Jim as he walked down the road to meet his buddy Bobby who was giving him the chance of a lifetime. As he passed Anna's house, she came running out the door, and he grabbed her and kissed her.

"Stop all that crying. I swear I will come back for you if it's the last thing I do, Lizzie, you hear me? So stop that crying."

"Write me, Jim. You write me every day," she pleaded with teary eyes.

"I can't write you every day, girl, but I promise I will write. I will send you a postcard of Cleveland." He laughed.

"Promise?"

"Promise."

Time passed, and Anna would check that mailbox every day looking to hear from Jim. She had even walked down and asked Joy if they had heard from him. But they had not. Several weeks later, Anna was walking home from school, and she began to feel dizzy and hot all over. She wasn't sure what was happening, and before she knew it, she was passed out in the middle of the road. Her friend Peggy was walking alongside her when it happened.

"Anna," she screamed

"Anna. Somebody help me, please."

Mr. Jenkins came running out his house hearing the cries.

"What happened?"

"I don't know. We were walkin' along, and all of a sudden, she was on the ground."

He ran in to get his wife, and as she came out, Anna had come to.

"Are you alright, sweetheart?" Mrs. Jenkins asked.

"I–I'm not sure," Anna responded, looking around. "I think so. I just felt dizzy all of a sudden, and everything just went sorta black and blurry. I think I'm okay."

Mrs. Jenkins took her up on the porch and got her some water, advising her to sit there for a while just to make sure.

"Do you think you're pregnant? I mean you did do it with Jim. Is your period late?" Peggy whispered to Anna as they sat in the rocking chairs on the front porch.

At that very moment, the reality of the fact that she might actually be pregnant hit her. She began to panic. She had not heard from Jim, she wasn't married, and her father would surely put her out. What was she going to do if she was? She had not even thought about her period being late.

"I just can't be. We only did it the one time. I don't think you can get pregnant from doing it just one time, can you?"

"Yes, you can," Peggy blurted out. "Don't be naïve, Anna. Everyone knows JoAnne only had sex one time with George, and that's why we don't see her no more. She somewhere havin' a baby."

"Peggy, I hope not." She stood nervously looking at Peggy. "I can't be, I just can't be."

But turned out, she was. Two days later, she and Peggy with the help of Peggy's older cousin, went two counties over to a doctor her cousin knew about. Peggy's cousin could use her husband's pickup, so she took them. She didn't have a driver's license, but that didn't matter. He would let her drive it anyway. On the ride home, Anna was quiet. Really, what was there to say? Peggy's cousin Linda tried to console her, but nothing she said made her feel any better. Her worse nightmare was coming true. How could she be so stupid?

"Well, honey, if you decide to get rid of it, I know a lady that can help. You will need fifty dollars."

"Fifty dollars! Where on God's green earth would I get fifty dollars?" Anna screamed. "This is a nightmare. A total nightmare." She began to cry and shake uncontrollably.

Peggy hopped over the seat and hugged her and cried with her. "I promise we will figure it out. You are not in this alone."

"Promises don't mean much, Peggy. Jim promised he would come back for me. It's been almost three months now, and I haven't even heard from him. I'm going to have to tell my dad. It's the only way I can get the money. He's going to kill me."

"Do you think he's going to let you get an abortion?"

"Well, I definitely don't think he's going to let me have a baby. Besides, if I don't hear from Jim, I'm going to apply to try and go to college."

The next day, she walked into the kitchen where her father sat drinking his morning coffee, reading the paper, eating grits and eggs. It was the longest walk and the hardest conversation she'd ever had. She had to muster up all the courage that was humanly possible.

"Daddy—" she looked over at him from the wall she was leaning on— "I, uh. I…" She began to shake.

"What is it? Are you okay?" He looked worried. "Where is your mother?"

"No, Daddy. I'm not okay. I'm so, so sorry. I didn't mean for this to happen. It's just that Jim was leaving, and it was the only one time, and I'm sorry Daddy. I'm so sorry."

"What? What are you saying?" His eyes filled with tears as his dreams for his baby girl seemed to fade. She never actually said the words, but he knew exactly what she was attempting to tell him, and his heart broke into too many pieces to count.

"How could you let this happen?" It wasn't anger or rage that came pouring out. It was sorrow. He held back the tears in his eyes. "We've worked so hard for you to have a better life, and you threw it away on Jim Holloway. Now he done skipped town and left you holdin' the bag."

"Daddy, it was just the one time, I swear. It was just the one time."

"Yes, yes. Just the one time. I heard you the first time you said it, but all it takes is one time as you can see."

"I just don't know what I was thinkin'. I just knew I was gonna miss him. I'm so sorry, Daddy, I didn't mean for this to happen," she cried out to him.

"No one ever does." He sighed. "No one ever does."

"There's a lady that can help."

She began to tell him about the lady that Peggy's cousin knew, but he knew it was unsafe, but knew there was no other way if she didn't want to keep the baby, not back then.

"We gotta talk to your momma about this. It's too much for me."

After discussing it further with her mother, her parents thought it would be best if she had the baby, but Anna didn't want to have the baby without Jim. She didn't want to be the average girl who

just had a bunch of babies and never got ahead. Her parents agreed to
help her with the baby and even keep the baby there if she wanted to
still go away to college. No matter what they said and all the
alternatives they came up with, she was not going to have that baby
without Jim there. So that was that, against their better judgement,
they agreed to let their baby girl go to the butcher, as her father called
her.

Anna called the number Peggy had written down for her.

"Hello," a woman answered.

"*Umm...ummm.* May I please speak to Madame Curry?"

"Yes, child. This is she."

"My best friend's cousin gave me your number. I need your
help as soon as possible."

"It will cost you fifty dollars. You alright with that, child?"

"Yes."

The next Saturday, her mom took her to see Madame Curry.
Her father sat on the porch saying goodbye in his mind to his little
girl. She had made a grown-up decision that lead her down a path that
could never be un-walked. She was his baby. How could this have
happened? Tears rolled down his cheeks as Anna and her mom
stepped out the front door. He would do anything to take this away
from her, but there was nothing he could do—nothing at all. Both her
parents looked at one another with an unspoken fear as they hoped for
the best that nothing would go wrong. He kissed Anna on the
forehead, promising her everything would be alright. He held his
wife's hand and walked her to the car, closing the door behind her as

she got in. He kissed her gently on the lips and stepped back. The car pulled slowly out of the driveway and headed for the ride of no return.

"Are you sure about this?"

"Yes."

"What if you are not able to have children after this?"

"It won't matter if Jim never comes back, now will it?"

"Anna."

"Mother, I really don't want to talk about this, okay? Anything but this."

"Okay. I understand." She sighed, and they rode in silence.

Anna stuck her arm out the window to feel the cool air as she wondered what Jim was doing while she was on her way to kill their baby.

They drove and drove, making their way down an unfamiliar dirt road, eventually turning onto a gravel driveway. There was a big house with a middle-aged Black woman who almost appeared White. She had her jet-black hair pulled into a tight bun, and you could see the various strands of gray hair throughout. Her skin looked soft as butter. She was beautiful, not scary or even spooky as Anna had envisioned by her name, Madame Curry. She stood as the car pulled in and approached the porch. Anna sat in the car until her mother came around and opened the door. She was scared but ready, but at the same time not ready. She still sat there even after the door was opened for her.

"Come on, honey." But Anna didn't budge. "You don't have to do this."

"Yes. Yes, I do." She swung one leg out of the car. It felt like lead. She scooted out of the car and dragged her weighted legs toward the porch.

"Good morning, my love." Madame Curry smiled a sort of comforting smile.

"Good morning," Anna and her mother said as they walked up the walkway.

"Sit. Sit. Before we start, I want to make sure this is something you absolutely have thought about and want to do, my child."

She took Anna by one hand and her mother by the other, but she looked directly into Anna's soul. "Once it's done, you cannot take it back. Children are a blessing, but you see it as a curse or you wouldn't be here. I just want to make sure you understand once I take your blessing from you, you may not be able to have other blessings. Sometimes this happens and you need to know this." She sighed. "This procedure shall we call it will cause some physical pain that will surely go away, but the pain in your head, your heart and your spirit may never go away." She looked at Anna, then her mother and then to Anna again.

Anna sat there speechless wondering if Madame Curry was there to help her or not.

"Look, I respect what you say, but I just can't have no baby. I just can't."

"If you could not bear a child young one, you would not be here. Say instead you wish not to do this thing." She stood and gathered her dress. "Come. You have fiery determination. Maybe it's better for you not to mother this child. Come let's go." She motioned for Anna to go through the door she was holding open.

As they entered her home, the smell of herbs and spices filled the atmosphere. It was surprisingly clean. There was a big kettle of water boiling, and she pointed Anna to a room at the rear of the house. She slowly opened the door and looked at the white walls and all the sterile tools laid out across a towel on the table. There was a wooden table similar to a dining table with padding covered in a stark white sheet.

"Undress, child, and put this on." She handed her a sheet. "Lay on the table. I will be right back." Anna did as she was told. Laying there on that table looking up into the ceiling of nothingness, she began to hate Jim. Where was he? How could he do this to her? There was no hope for redemption. She had made up in her mind laying on that table that other than death, there was nothing he could ever say or do to change this thing that was changing her life forever.

Anna's mother waited nervously in the living room.

"This will relax you. She will be alright." Madame Curry handed her a cup of tea. "You, love, are a good mother. Don't you forget that. Let this not be the weight that tips the scale in any other direction. Do you understand me?"

She waited for a response before turning and re-entering the room where Anna lay waiting.

She explained she was giving her something to help her relax but that she would feel the majority of the procedure. "I am just going to help you start and allow nature to take its course. Now take a deep breath."

She was right. Anna felt some pain and let out a scream, which startled her mother, causing her to drop the tea cup. Madame Curry heard the cup shatter. She called out, "Everything is fine, love. She is alright, expected pain. Don't worry about the cup. I will clean it up later."

Anna chanted, "I'm okay, I'm okay, I'm okay" as she squeezed her eyes shut tightly. "I hate you, Jim. I curse the day I ever met you. You are a liar. A liar, I tell you." She breathed, she cried, she cramped, she screamed, and when everything was completed, Madame Curry explained how to care for herself the next several days. She advised her to lay there and rest a while, and she gave her some pain medication.

Madame Curry and Anna's mother sat in the living room talking about life and decisions and living with them. About two hours later, Anna made her way up to the door.

"I'm ready to go." She leaned on the wall, holding herself.

They both stood. "Did you bring the blanket I told you to?"

She looked at Anna, but her mother answered. "Yes. We have it in the car."

"I want you to lay it across the backseat and let her cover herself to stay warm, and just let her lay down in the back and rest the ride home."

She nodded, and they both helped her out to the car and got her comfortable. Before closing the door, Madame Curry stooped down, rubbing Anna's head and spoke gently but passionately, with conviction. "Listen, darling, you have done this thing. Now I want you to put it behind you and live a life that will make you not regret this decision, or it will never be worth it."

She didn't wait for Anna to respond. She stood, turned and walked back to the house. She stood on the porch and waved as they left, and that was the last she saw of Madame Curry. She vowed she would never return.

Anna sat up and rolled her window down. "Madame Curry," Anna called to her. "I will make it worth it. I am going to do something with my life that will make a difference."

In April, she got her acceptance letter to college. Three weeks later, she got a letter from Jim.

Dear Lizzie,

Sorry I am just writing. Life has been real busy here. I work a lot of hours and have been saving up my money. Things have not been happening as fast as I hoped, but I will send for you soon. I think you will really like it here. There is a lot to do. It's different here than the South. Blacks have more opportunity here. Anyway. I will let you know when I'mma send for you.

Love,
Jim

When she read the letter, there were a host of emotions: excitement, anger, resentment. She pulled out a sheet of paper and began to write furiously.

Dearest Jim,

I don't know what you expect me to say nearly seven months later. Life has changed—in fact it has changed me. You changed me. My heart is and will be forever broken. When you first left, every day I came home and checked the mail, hopin' and prayin' to hear from you, the man who said he loved me and would come back for me. The one who said he would write to me. I never got one letter. Neither did your family. I needed you, Jim, and you were not here. I was pregnant and alone. I didn't know what to do or if you were even comin' back. I had to kill our baby, Jim, because you left me with no hope. Now I have to go live with purpose. I cannot let my baby's death be in vain.

I gotta go make something of myself. After I didn't hear from you, I applied to college, and guess what? I got in, so I'm going.

I'm goin', Jim, and my baby's gonna be lookin' down from heaven smilin', watchin' over me.

Take care of yourself, Jim. I hope Cleveland is treatin' you mighty fine. Cleveland took you away from me. Cleveland changed my life, and I ain't never even been there.

Love,

Anna

Jim never got over that, and he was too stubborn to chase after her. After all, he is God's gift.

"Off to college after she done killed my baby," he mumbled to himself when he read her letter. He balled it up and threw it in the trash, but later went back and retrieved it. He was going to show her. He wrote her, telling her to stop that foolish talk and come be with him in maybe another six months or so, but she never wrote back. He had already broken her heart, and she had already decided she would not live for a man.

She did well too—finished college and left Mississippi. She did what she once thought was impossible. She eventually met a man who swept her off her feet, and they settled down and had three beautiful children. She and Peggy were still best friends, and she came home to visit her parents every chance she got. They were so proud of her. So maybe the most painful thing in her life turned into her power. And that was the story of Anna Elizabeth Jackson. Jim never recovered from this, and he buried that pain deep down within. He had loved her so much.

As Jim's family filled their ears with stories of their life in Mississippi, Josephine and the girls sat back in their chairs amazed at the man they were hearing about. "I didn't think Daddy was capable of loving anyone but himself." June smirked.

They were all puzzled. They sensed the tension and disconnect from the girls.

"Is everything alright, Josephine?" Ruth asked.

"*Hmm.* Yes, Ruth. All is well."

She got up from the table and went upstairs to her room. She had to deal with the fact that Jim must have loved Anna. Why would he still have her picture?

What she didn't know was that Jim had actually written several letters to Anna after receiving her letter, begging her to give him another chance. He was pained she had an abortion and felt foolish he had not taken time to write her, but he was embarrassed things had not come together as quickly as he had hoped, and secretly he was enjoying that single city life. He never mailed any of the letters because he thought it would make him look weak, so he let the woman he truly loved get away.

He knew he could never replace her. Josephine was good initially, but she was no Anna, and she was definitely no Jane. She never had a chance of real love from Jim. If only she had known, maybe her life could have been different too.

How do you measure up to a ghost you never knew existed? Here she was thinking Jim didn't know how to love, that he was so broken he lacked the capacity and was doing the best he could. Turns out that wasn't it at all. He was just incapable of loving her. Her heart ached even more as she realized it wasn't just Jane she was competing with. That, she thought she understood. He just wanted a White woman, just had to have one to feel accomplished, but here Anna was, and she wasn't White—she was Black too—so why did he love her and not Josephine after all she did to try and make him happy?

She leaned against the wall in the room, staring at herself in the mirror, wondering where Josephine was and when she had lost her. She felt embarrassed loving Jim the way she did, always hoping it would get better only to find out it never would,

Downstairs, the kids enjoyed meeting their aunts and uncles, and of course Ruth. They were a little saddened Jim's dad was no longer around, so they never had a chance to meet the man they heard so many stories about that weekend. Wow, how much they had missed out on with Jim keeping them separated from his family. They continued to remain in disbelief because their father seemed like he was so much fun growing up, and they didn't know that part of him. They knew the monster he had become. Each of them deep down longed for a good dad, but they were dealt a different hand, and no matter how much they heard these stories they could not reconcile the two men.

The Funeral

The morning of the funeral, Josephine sat on the bed talking to a picture of Jim.

"Well, you mean bastard, this is it. This is our final goodbye. I loved you, Jim. You hear that? I loved you so much, but I don't anymore. I am glad you're gone because now I'm free. Free, you hear me? Free! I hope you're free too. All the hell you gave me, I still hope the little piece of God you had was enough for Him to let you in. Now, maybe you're someplace where you'll know what love truly is. My new life will be a scary, different challenge, but I'll no longer be under your thumb. The challenge will be learning how to live—to live my life without you. The challenge will be to find out who I am."

She glanced over at the mirror, barely recognizing who she had become. "Who are you, Josephine Lilly Holloway? Who are you?" she screamed at the top of her lungs. She laughed, then cried then laughed again. "Well, I guess we 'bouta find out, ain't we?" she said in the voice of her mother.

Her belly was filled with laughter, yet burned with fear. She wondered how her stomach could be all tied up in knots and feel a tinge of happiness all at once.

Honey was going to get her mom when she heard her mother talk and scream and laugh and cry and then take a huge breath. So, she hung back for a moment and waited for a quiet to come.

"Alright, Jim, let's get this over with." Josephine stood courageously to put her lipstick on but her hand shook. "Come on, hand. Work. I don't have time for nerves."

She pressed the tube hard to her lips and forced it on straight and headed toward the door.

Honey opened it as if she was just walking up. "Hey, Momma. You ready?"

"Yes baby. Ready as I will ever be, I guess."

Honey put her arm through Josephine's, and they walked down the stairs together. "It's better for us, Momma." Honey looked over at Josephine with tears in her eyes. "Okay, just remember that. Him being gone is best for everybody."

Josephine knew this was true, but it still hurt deep in her soul. She always hoped one day if she was perfect enough and tried to be everything Jim needed, it would be how it was when they first met— or at least be okay. She wanted to be happy, but she wanted to be happy with Jim. That never happened, and now it never would, and she just didn't know how to be okay with that.

Everyone gathered round in the living room, waiting for the limousine to arrive. Ruth wanted to have prayer before they went to the church, so they did. She cried during prayer, but not a whole lot. She said in some ways it was as if Jim had been gone a long time ago and she had made her peace with the fact that he didn't want to have anything to do with her and their family. Even though she had done this, she knew he was alive. Now she had to work through the permanency of the death of her son and the fact that she was losing him all over again.

The limousine ride to the church was completely silent. Joy attempted to make a small joke, which was not received well and all conversation came to a close. As they pulled up toward the church, the parking lot was full, and cars lined the street.

"My goodness," Ruth said. "Are all these people here for my Jim? He must've really been somebody. That was always important to Jim. Looks like he found what he was chasing."

"He was somebody alright." Diane rolled her eyes.

"Jo," Jim Jr. said, using his name for her, "you are not going to let her disrespect Dad like that, are you?"

"Why are you calling your mother Jo, Jim Jr.?" Ruth looked stunned.

"Because that's her name, Ruth," he responded sarcastically.

"That's enough. I will not have that today. Show some respect for the dead," Josephine blurted.

"Why?" Diane questioned. "He sure didn't show us any. You are his wife, and he had more respect for the people outside our house than in it. I guess you are going to be his wife 'til the end, huh? Still taking up for him, making excuses. You don't have to do that anymore, Momma. He's gone. Gone. Wherever he is, he can't hurt you anymore, so you don't have to be scared, and you don't have to defend him." She let out a loud sigh of frustration. "Hurry up and let me out of this car." She crawled over June and Ruth to escape as soon as the car stopped.

Diane was so mad she felt tears rising up, but she refused to let one fall. She didn't want anyone to see her and think it was because she was sad Jim was gone. He did not deserve one tear, not one. Her tears were fiery angry rage that was built up and wanted out.

Josephine refused to look at Ruth and carried on as if that scene had not just transpired.

Ruth was beginning to wonder who her son had become and just what was looming at the underbelly of this household. Growing up in Mississippi, Jim's family may not have had a whole lot, but they had love, and disrespect was one thing that was never tolerated in their home.

"Okay, everyone—" Josephine took a deep breath—"Let's do our best to be strong. Walk with your heads held high. Let's go."

They each filed out of the limo one by one on both sides before gathering themselves and lining up. As they walked into the church, Jim stepped in front of Josephine, and as Diane went to snatch him, Josephine grabbed her hand.

"Let it be."

So, they entered in, Jim Jr., Josephine, Honey, Diane, June, Ruth, Sam, Joy, Robert and Hazel. The church was completely packed—standing room only. The faces were all a blur to Josephine though she had known quite a few of these people most of her adult life. Many of them got up and said the most beautiful things about Jim.

Diane could not help but wonder how he had them all so fooled. The man they described was nothing like the man they knew.

There were even several White people at the funeral who spoke very highly of Jim. This really impressed Ruth and his siblings. This was just not common—in fact, almost unheard of where they came from.

It was all a fog to Josephine. That is until it was time for people to walk around for one final viewing of Jim and pay their respects to the family. The fog began to lift as this one woman, beautiful and elegant, walking with a young boy appearing to be eight maybe nine came into her view. The little boy began to cry as they passed the casket. The woman bent over shushing him with a soft, comforting voice as she wiped his tears.

"It's going to be okay, sweetie. I promise." She pushed her sunglasses back up snuggly to her face and looked over at Josephine as she walked past.

It was all moving in exponentially slow time. Josephine's brain began to go into overdrive with questions. *Is that Jane?* she thought. But before she could wrap her head around what was happening and come up with answers to her own questions.

"Who was that?" Ruth whispered to June.

"I don't know. Never seen her before. Jim knew a lot of people though, so it could anybody."

"Hmmm," Ruth mumbled, sensing something not quite right with the woman. But she had to admit whoever she was, she was quite beautiful. She was a soft golden white, if there is such a thing, not pale or pink. Her skin was beautiful, and her shiny, bouncy blond curls draped across her shoulders. Her lips were colored a deep pink, which was a bit much for a funeral, but it sure made her lips pop.

There was no way this woman could walk passed and people not take notice. Her large breasts pushed up out the top of that dress and her tiny doll-like waist was in perfect symmetry to the rest of her body. Definitely no way to go unnoticed.

Josephine wanted so badly to run after her and find out if in fact that was Jane and if so, question the audacity of her coming and showing her adulteress face, but how could she? Jim had invited her there—invited her into their lives whether she liked it or not. She felt comfortable enough to waltz in there, and with a child no less. Who brings a child to a funeral if they aren't family? A child? Wait, a child? If that was Jane, Josephine paused thinking to herself, *Could? No.* Jim wouldn't sink that low, but if not, then who was the child? Who could easily be of mixed race. Who was that child? Who? She kept screaming in her head.

Josephine's heart began to race, and her palms began to feel clammy. *How much more hurt can I be expected to take?* she thought. She saw why Jim wouldn't want to come home to her when he was layin' up with that. It made her feel even worse then she already did. Her eyes held the tears hostage until they could no longer maintain the wall, and they escaped down her cheeks, dropping onto her black suit jacket. She remembered what it was like to be beautiful. To have people stare when she walked into a room. Jim had taken that from her and given it to Jane. After standing by him, loving him, birthing his children, and still she was never going to be enough.

Of course people thought the tears were for Jim, which made Ruth happy believing Josephine loved her son that much, but in all actuality, the tears were for herself. The self she had lost so many years ago.

June turned to Diane. "Who is that lady?"

"I don't know, but I'm going to find out."

June pulled her arm close as she made an attempt to go after the woman. "No, Diane, just wait. Now is not the time."

"We may never see her again. Now is exactly the time." She yanked away from June and stood.

"Where are you off to?" Josephine questioned Diane as if she didn't already know. She knew. They all had the same question she was pondering, Diane was just the only one courageous enough to find out.

"I'll be right back, Momma. Promise." She looked at Josephine with sheer determination to find out who this woman was. She had a feeling it was not good and that was why she had to go. Josephine was glad she had gone, not that it mattered now, but she still wanted to know if that was the woman Jim chose to love more than her.

Jim and Jane

J ane was never meant to be more than a symbol of validation. Jim initially carried such a hatred for Whites, especially White men, and Jane was a way to get back at them. Over time, he softened a little toward Whites due to his relationship with Paul. He was different. He treated Jim with respect, and they worked well together and developed an uncommon friendship. That chance meeting outside the bank that day made a difference in both men's lives. But it was almost too late. The success of White men continued to cause Jim to slowly hate himself. He tried over and over to prove he was as good as them. The root of every calculated decision made in his life could always be traced back to the helpless little boy who could not stand up to the White man who had the power to take anything he wanted, including his momma, and he and his Daddy could do nothing about it. Times were changing, but they had not changed so that Jim would ever be equal to a White man, and he knew it, and it tore a hole through his soul. It did not matter how many Black men, and women for that matter, looked up to him and thought him to be accomplished. It just wasn't enough and never would be.

So what better way to get back at them than by one, becoming successful and two, being able to give it to a White girl—at least that's what he told Bobby at the bar one night with a cigarette hanging from his lip as he squinted his right eye to combat the smoke that entered it.

"They did it to us—stole our women, raped and disrespected them and us, right to our faces—and we couldn't do nothin' about it. Nothin'. Had us lookin' like a bunch of cowards. At least Jane comin' willingly. I don't have to do nothin' but call, and she freely gives it all to me. I ain't gotta take nothin'."

"But you disrespectin' Josephine like she ain't nobody, just like the White man would."

"Ain't nobody disrespectin' no Jo. I take care of my house. What I do outside it ain't her business."

"If you say so, but I don't know why you gotta be messin' around on her. She's a good woman."

"You know, Bobby, we just see things different, you and me. You know you movin' up in the world when you got a woman as fine as Jane givin' you the eye. I knew she wanted me, I could tell. Every time I go up to the office, she finds a reason to walk past me in those tight skirts and her boobs screaming to get out those tight sweaters. Well, I had decided I was gonna let 'em out, and she was gon' let me. I could already tell." He laughed to himself, put his cigarette down and threw back another shot.

"Man, why you wanna do that? Josephine probably one of the finest women you ever gon' meet, and she chose you, man. Outta all the men she coulda had, she chose you. It ain't right, Jim. Josephine a good woman. She don't deserve that."

"Aw, man, shut up. What you know? You just mad you ain't got one sniffin' up behind you."

"Naw, man, I love my beautiful Black woman. The darker the berry, the sweeter the juice. You can keep the milky whites." Bobby leaned back on the barstool and let out a hearty laugh.

"Well, Bob, yo' loss. Milk does a body good! Whew, yes it does."

They both laughed loudly before each taking one more shot and heading to their respective homes.

That pretty much sums up the illogical beginning of the relationship that grew into Jim actually falling in love with Jane. It wasn't in his plan. He just wanted to have sex with her and boast about it, but turns out, she was kindhearted and funny and did things in the bedroom he had never experienced before. Josephine was a virgin when he met her, so everything she knew he taught her, but Jane had a little experience, and she wasn't afraid to try stuff— anything she thought would make Jim love her. The weight of the world wasn't on him when he was with Jane. He wasn't a Black man. He was just a man—her man—and she made him feel every bit of a man. Life was hard trying to make your way in a world that rejected you, and when he lay in Jane's arms and she stroked his head, he was unguarded. He didn't have to fight, just relax and be loved.

For Jane, it was an adventure. She was always one to push boundaries if for no other reason than to get a response, and though not many people knew of her and Jim's relationship, the few who did never really approved but what could she do? She lost a really good friend who just could not fathom her willingly allowing a Black man to touch her, especially touch her in her most intimate places. She thought Jane was nasty and wanted nothing more to do with her. It bothered Jane initially—they had been friends since grade school, She just begged her not to tell her parents because at that point Jane's parents didn't know, and she knew if she told her parents, they would indeed tell Jane's parents and who knows, they may have no longer wanted to associate with her family. It was complicated, but he was worth it.

Stacy and Jessica hung in there with her and tried not to judge and secretly wished they were bold enough to try something so daring, but since neither of them were, they continued to live through the stories Jane was always so eager to share. She, of course like Jim, never planned on falling in love with him. This was just for fun—at least that's what it was supposed to be. But the initially hard romps in the bed turned to delicate kisses, hand holding and life sharing experiences that neither of them saw coming and everything else that comes along with building intimacy. They shared everything—there were hardly any secrets between the two. Jim, of course, held back some things, but for the most part, if it was in his heart or happened in his life, Jane was usually the one he shared it with. He told her things that not even Bobby knew. Things he thought would make him look like a punk, he would say. Jane made him feel like it was okay to feel the soft side that he sometimes needed to express. He had to be tough for life and all it threw his way but not for Jane.

They often talked about moving overseas to a place they might be more accepted so they could get married and love publicly, but they knew that would never happen. She begged him to leave

Josephine, but he couldn't. His image would not recover from that type of scandal in his church, and image was everything to Jim. He lived his life based on the person he had created outside his home. He had a good life, and he knew it—why go making it harder than it had to be? Jane had no idea how much of his affection she truly had. She was always jealous of Josephine. Had she known the truth of his marriage, the truth of the other Jim, she may have been careful as to what she was wishing for.

She wanted it all, even though Jim spent a lot money and time on her. She wanted more time. It was never enough and always seemed to be cut short because he never spent the night away from home for his foolishness with Jane. She would beg and plead, but it was always a no-go, and that made her resent Josephine even more. She was tired of being the other woman. She wanted him all to herself. She wanted to wake up in his arms and cook breakfast and not feel cheap as she often did whenever Jim left. She could never make him understand that even though his words expressed his love and affection, words could only go so far. He told her he didn't love Josephine and that she had all his love, but love would not keep him there with her.

One night, as he got up to leave—it was about one a.m.—Jane grabbed his arm and pleaded with him not to go. She tried kissing him and attempting to arouse him again thinking at least if they had more sex he would stay longer, but it didn't work.

"Jane. Jane, stop. Man, I already told you I have to go. That's enough. I done already been here way longer than I should have."

"Come on, baby. You know you want this."

"I already got it, girl. Now I gotta go."

"Come on, Jim. Please don't leave me. I get tired of sleeping alone. I want a normal relationship like all my other friends. It's bad enough I deal with the fact that you're Black. That already puts pressure on us, but then you being married makes it even worse. It's like I'm the double dirty secret, and I'm tired of it. I'm better than this, Jim, and I deserve more." Her eyes filled with tears as she clung to his arm in desperation.

Jim pulled back, shaking her grip from him, "What you trying to say, Jane? Huh? You knew what this was when you let me in your bed. Don't try to change it up now. Quit tellin' your little friends everything and comparing yourself to 'em. What we got ain't never gonna be normal. If you was lookin' for normal, you woulda kept walkin' passed me. Now stop all that crying, I ain't gonna come over here and deal with this." He looked at her sternly. "I mean it, Jane. I ain't gon' do it."

"Just this one night, baby, please. I need you to be here with me. Just one night." Her voice was weak and pathetic, and she knew it. "What do I have to do, baby? Please just tell me, and I'll do it. I need you."

Jim finished dressing and walked out without so much as a look in her direction. He didn't want to look her in her eyes. Deep down, he didn't want to let her down, but he wasn't about to start allowing her to dictate what he would or would not be doing. He was guiding this ship, and he couldn't afford to have a co-captain, not even Jane.

He sat in the car discretely parked and slammed his hands down hard on the steering wheel. He didn't mean to be so cold toward Jane. He had no intentions of hurting her, but who did she think she was? She wasn't gonna be making demands on him. That was not going to happen, and the sooner she realized it, the better things would be. If he started giving in every time she begged or cried, he would no longer be in control, and he wasn't having that.

It didn't matter though because Jane had a trick up her sleeve Jim never saw coming, the oldest trick in the book: pregnancy. For several months, she did nothing to prevent pregnancy. Jim had never worried about it because Jane was on the pill, and he trusted her, but she was growing tired of things being the way they were. She needed to up the ante in her favor. Finally, after months of conniving and plenty of sex, which Jim enjoyed every bit of, she missed her period.

Now, most unwed women would be devastated in her situation during these times, but not Jane. She could not wait to go to the doctor and make a spectacle of herself if it meant getting more leverage with Jim.

Finally, the day came for her appointment, and she was right: She was indeed pregnant. The doctor asked her about the father, and she implied he was not a part of her life. She knew she risked being ostracized as the doctor and nurse both turned and looked at each other with disapproving pity.

"Well, did you want to consider other options?" the nurse asked delicately.

"Oh no. Of course not. I could never." Jane was offended at the thought, let alone the actual suggestion to complete such a hideous act. She thought, If only they knew how she had tried and tried to get pregnant with Jim's child, they would not even be asking such a thing.

"Things happen. There's nothing to be ashamed of, but you don't want to ruin your life." The nurse placed her hand over Jane's.

"And you want to be able to get a husband and have children the right way, don't you?" the doctor expressed himself sternly.

"I'll be fine. I just want to go now."

She was beginning to realize she hadn't really thought this through, and now she had to find the courage to tell Jim. She had no idea how he would react, but she just hoped he would be happy, and this could be what they needed to push their relationship in the right direction. She decided it would be best to wait and tell him in a public place because she knew he wouldn't make a scene. Jim never wanted people to think he didn't have it all together, so no matter what he was feeling, he would be calm, and that's what she wanted, good or bad. People would already be staring because she was White, but she was used to that by then.

The first couple of years, they never went out in public but as their relationship grew, and they got more comfortable, there were a few places they would and were allowed to go. People would stare, but they were used to it, and it didn't bother Jane as much as it did initially. It never really bothered Jim. He was proud to flaunt his trophy, usually in places where he wasn't well known.

The night she finally got up the nerve to tell him, Jim had invited her out to a jazz club they frequented. His work life and church life didn't know this side of Jim. Here at the club, they knew Jane, and even though many didn't approve—mainly the women— they could let their hair down there. No one was rude to them there but Black women felt slighted, him bringing Barbie in their faces, when there were so many good Black women.

The whole time Jane was getting ready, she played out various scenarios of how she would tell him and how he would receive the news. Of course she wanted him to be happy, but she knew that was unrealistic, but she just hoped it wouldn't end their relationship. She brushed her hair and powdered her face. She put on Jim's favorite red dress and the perfect shade of red lipstick. Just as she was putting her shoes on, there was the buzzer. She took a deep breath and headed to the door. She buzzed him in and unlocked the door. He came in as she was getting her clutch and her shawl.

"You look beautiful. Turn around. Let me look at you." He spun her around, checking her out. "Yes, Lord. You know you're the most beautiful woman on this earth, girl." He pulled her to him and softly kissed her lips, in an attempt not to get lipstick all over his face. "You know, that's my favorite dress. You must want somethin'." He chuckled, but didn't care because whatever she asked for, he always made a way to get it for her. "You all ready?"

"Yes, baby. I sure am."

Jim opened the door, and they made their way to the club.

"Hey, Jim. What's it doin' tonight?"

"Aww, man Cliff, nothin', man. Not a thing," he said, laughing. There was a table for him near the front, off to the side. They usually sat him there when Jane was with him because it was a little darker and gave them a little more privacy. But for as much as they liked privacy, Jim's chest was stuck far out, and he walked like he was ten feet tall as he pranced Jane through to the front. It was usually the women who disapproved as the men gave secret nods of approval. The waitress came around to get their drink order.

"Glass of red wine and a shot of whiskey."

"Oh, no, I'm not going to have anything to drink tonight."

"What? Are you sure? Why not? You're not feeling okay?"

"I'm fine. Just club soda, please."

"You think I'mma get you drunk and take advantage of you," Jim said jokingly. "You sure you okay?'

"Yes, Jim baby, I'm fine."

He pulled her close to him as they listened to his boy Ray on the horn, giving the people what they wanted. Jim loved music—he always had. It took him to a different place. He didn't know which he loved to escape to more, the music or Jane. Both were a much-needed sanctuary for him, and he indulged. As the night went on, they laughed and talked and let the music carry them away.

"You look like you got something on ya mind. What is it? I knew that dress had a secret." He smiled and leaned into her face. "Spill it."

Jane leaned in as well and took his hand under the table. She nervously said his name, soft and low. She cleared her throat. "Jim baby, I have something I need to tell you."

"What is it, honey? What's wrong? You look like you seen a ghost or somethin'."

"Jim, you know I love you, and I know you love me, and I didn't mean for this to happen, I just don't know how it happened." Her voice began to shake. As sure as she thought this was a good idea when she stopped taking her birth control pills, now that she was faced with telling Jim she was pregnant, it no longer seemed so great.

Suddenly the band seemed miles away in the smoke-filled room. "What is it, Jane? You're scaring me, girl." Jim turned and began to scoot away from her. He thought maybe she wanted to break things off. "Listen, Jane, I ain't got time for all this, now spit it out. You tryin' to tell me you wanna leave me? You didn't mean for it to happen? You got somebody else? Is that what this is about?" She sat in silence. "Huh?" he barked. "Is it? 'Cause I ain't havin' it. You mine, Jane. That's it, and that's all. You are mine!"

"No, Jim," she blurted out. "It's…it's…*ummm*…well…" She let out a huge sigh. "I'm pregnant, Jim. There, there it is: I'm pregnant."

Jim jumped up. "What the hell, Jane? How could you let this happen?"

"Jim baby, sit down. Don't make a scene."

Jim sat in the chair and shook his head in disbelief. "Are you sure?"

"Yes, I'm sure. I went to the doctor this week. I just didn't know how to tell you, and I didn't want to tell you over the phone."

"We talked about this, and I told you this couldn't happen. You promised me this wouldn't happen. Ain't you on that pill they got?"

"Yes, Jim, but nothing is one hundred percent guaranteed, and you sure don't seem worried every time you want to come lay between my thighs." He grabbed his wallet and threw some money on the table to take care of the bill and for Jane to get home.

"Catch a cab. I ain't dealing with this right now." He turned to walk out.

"Jim, wait," she called after him in a loud whisper.

"Don't, Jane. Don't follow me."

He headed to the phone booth to call Bobby.

Jane sat there at the table of the smoky club. The tears filled her eyes. She didn't want anyone to see her cry, but she was stuck in the quicksand of that seat, paralyzed, nowhere to hide from herself even if she wasn't.

"Excuse me," she called to the waitress. "I will take that glass of wine." She sat there another thirty minutes or so before walking to the front and asking Cliff if he could call a cab for her.

"You alright, Miss Jane?"

She sighed, laughed and teared up all at once before nodding.

Jim dialed Bobby's number and waited as the phone rang Bobby's wife answered, "Hey, it's Jim. Is Bobby there?"

Soon after, Bobby picked up.

"Hey, Can you meet me at Charlie's for a drink? I need to talk to you."

"You alright, man?"

"Yeah, man. You gon' meet me or not?" Jim sounded agitated.

"Yeah, I'll be there in a minute, man. This better not be no BS." He hung up and headed for the door, letting his wife know he was going to meet Jim.

"Everything alright?" she asked.

"Who knows? It's Jim." He chuckled.

When Bobby arrived at the bar, he spotted Jim downing a shot, chasing it with a beer. He was dressed like he had been out on the town. He knew this was not going to be good. He walked up and motioned to the bartender for a shot of whiskey as he sat next to his clearly distraught friend.

He slapped Jim on the back. "What's going on, man?"

"She's pregnant, man. Dammit, Bobby, Jane done messed around and got herself pregnant."

"Well, man, she ain't do it by herself. What did you expect? How long y'all thought y'all was gonna do this without something goin' wrong? God see everything, Jim. I told you to leave that girl alone. She probably did it on purpose. Them type know exactly what they be doin', and now you the fool. Shoot, what you gon' do now? What if Jo finds out?"

"What if? What she gonna do? She just gon' deal with it. I ain't worried about Jo, man. What people gonna think of me cheating on her and getting another woman pregnant? That's what I'm concerned about, not Jo."

"I ain't gon' never understand you, Jim. Never. Nothing is never enough for you. I knew this would come back to bite you, but here you is thinkin' you untouchable. No matter how good you got it, you gon' always find a way to have to have more, no matter who it hurt or what it cost. Here you are still worried about yourself. Nobody but Jim matters."

"Hopefully Jane gets rid of it, Bobby, and then nobody gotta worry about nothin'."

Bobby sucked his teeth. "See what I mean? That's dangerous, man." Bobby showed his disapproval.

"What I'm supposed to do, just let her prance around here carrying my baby? I don't think so, man. Ain't no other choice unless you got some better options. What would you do?"

"Man, I would never be in your position 'cause I ain't never, ever, ever cheating on my wife. She would kill me, I could tell. She a good woman, but she got a crazy streak." He shook his head. "She even said it before while she was in the kitchen choppin' onions, and when she pointed that knife toward me and asked me if I understood that she had no problem killing me if I ever cheated on her, I was crystal clear." Bobby chuckled, trying to make light of the situation.

"*Awww,* man, you a sissy. Who wear the pants over there? I'm beginning to think it shole ain't you."

"Huh, she can wear the pants, the dresses, draws and anything else she want. That woman is good to me and good for me. You got the same thing, just too fool to know it."

They sat and talked and cracked a few more jokes in between Bobby giving Jim the business about his stupidity, but in the end, the truth still had to be dealt with, and no matter how much he talked to Bobby, it wasn't going to change the reality of his situation.

He lay in the bed next to Josephine that night wondering why he was the way he was with her. He thought about the things Bobby had said about her being a good woman and all, but still, he couldn't see her as enough. She didn't seem to be much of anything these days. There was no excitement in their relationship. She no longer seemed to worship the ground he walked on as she once did. Deep down, he knew it was partly his fault, but it had gone on too long, and there was too much distance between them now to think things could ever be right. He was obligated to stay, not just for them but for him. But there were many days when all he wanted to do was run—run like he ran away from Mississippi—and never looked back. At times he felt like he was suffocating, dying to escape from himself, his life, and the mess he created. From the outside, he had it all together, but deep down inside, he hated himself almost as much as he hated his father for not being different, for settling for what the White man said he could have.

He began to breathe fast. His heart was racing, and he began to sweat profusely. He jumped out of bed, stumbled down the stairs and sat out on the porch. He took some deep breaths, and for the first time, he asked God to help him. He looked up at the sky and asked why he had to be born who he was and why he had to fight so much harder to get what he got.

"It ain't fair, God. You hear me? It ain't fair." The anger turned into sobs as he fell onto the steps crying out to the invisible almighty he had heard so much about but never really knew. Church was something he did as part of his persona, but it wasn't who he was.

He sat there and watched the sun come up. Soon, Josephine woke up and saw Jim's side of the bed had been slept on, and she wondered where he was that early on Saturday morning, especially after being out drinking. She pulled herself from the bed and grabbed a robe and walked down the hall to brush her teeth and wipe her face. She went to the kitchen, but there was no Jim. As she walked into the living room, she caught a glimpse of him sitting on the front steps in his pajamas for all the neighborhood to see. She opened the door and spoke to him softly through the screen.

"Hey, there you are. You alright, Jim?"

"Yeah, Josephine. I feel fine, just needed some air."

"Well, do you need anything?"

"Just some coffee."

"Alright." She closed the door and went off to the kitchen to make the coffee. When it was done, she walked it out onto the porch and handed it off to him. "You sure everything alright, Jim? Your mind looks heavy."

"I said I'm alright. Now go on back in the house in your night clothes."

He sat there a few more hours before getting dressed for the day. Normally on Saturdays he and Josephine went to the grocery store and then he did a little yardwork. After that, he hit the streets or Jane's, but not today. He cut the grass and sat on the couch watching television the majority of the day. Didn't even eat breakfast or lunch and picked over dinner. Josephine knew there was something wrong, but she dared not ask again for fear it might set Jim off, and as long as he wasn't bothering her, she was fine, and she wanted to keep it that way.

All that day, Jim pondered what exactly he was to do. He couldn't simply turn his back on Jane. She had come to mean so much to him. He didn't mean to hurt her, but she needed to understand how serious he was about not having a baby with her or anyone else for that matter. He loved women, but hated them at the same time. He loved when they obeyed him and became what he needed them to be whether it was a lover or a punching bag, and that's just the way it was.

On the other side of town, Jane didn't come out the house for several days. What had she done, and how could she make it right between them? She loved Jim and just wanted to make sure he wasn't going anywhere. *How could I be so stupid?* She played that tune over and over in her head. She was afraid to tell anyone out of sheer embarrassment, not knowing if Jim would be around or not. She couldn't keep any food down, but she wasn't sure if it was because of the baby or the nerves she was experiencing of the uncertainty of what life would be for her and this baby who was unwanted by its own father. She cried herself to sleep most nights, and during the day she wanted to talk to Jim so bad.

By the sixth day, she knew she had to pull herself together. She turned on the radio that morning really loud and showered for almost thirty minutes.

"We're going to be alright, you and me. I promise. She got dressed for work and decided she wouldn't worry about it anymore until she began to show and would have to explain to people what was going on. The longer she went without hearing from Jim, the more she felt abandoned. She couldn't believe he was able to just walk away as if she didn't matter.

Several weeks passed before Jim was ready to deal with Jane and the situation. He sat in the living room watching television and drinking beer until everyone had gone to bed for the night. When Jim drank, it pretty much isolated everyone, so it wasn't long before they had all vanished upstairs. A little after midnight, he made his way into the kitchen to dial Jane up. The phone rang several times, but he didn't hang up. He waited. He knew she was home—where else would she be pregnant at midnight and without him? He knew good and well she knew better than to be out that late without him.

"Hello," Jane answered in a sleepy voice.

"Hey," Jim whispered.

"Jim!" She was excited to hear him on the other end. He had completely cut her off since she had told him about the baby, yet she was excited for any bone he tossed her way.

"Hey, uh, did you arrange to take care of that?"

"Arrange to take care of what?"

"The baby. You know what."

"Jim, I cannot believe you're asking me to kill my baby." She began to sob uncontrollably. "I can't do that. I just can't."

"You can and you will, Jane. Now hush up all that crying. I ain't got time for your foolish fairytale thinking. What you think gonna happen? Huh? You think I'mma leave my family and come raise that baby with you? 'Cause I'm not gon' do it. You hear me, Jane? I'm not. I got too much to lose. So the best thing for you to do for both of us is to get rid of it, and things can go back to the way they were."

"You don't have to do a thing, Jim. I won't ask you for anything if that's how you want it." Her voice shook with tears.

"Jane, I'm just saying, use your head."

"Jim, I'm tired, and I'm going back to bed." She hung the phone up. She didn't say it angrily or tearfully, just very matter-of-fact.

"Jane. Jane," he whispered loudly into the phone receiver. His drunken state didn't let him ignore the realization of what had just transpired. He stood solemnly for a moment in pure disbelief she had actually hung up on him. He called back several times and got no answer, which caused anger to kindle within him. Before he knew it, he was grabbing his keys, sliding on his shoes and heading straight for her apartment.

Josephine heard the car start up and went to the window in time to see him pulling out the driveway. She wondered where he was going this time of night. Jim was good for staying out late but not leaving the house at this hour. She figured it had something to do with the way he had been acting the last few weeks, but she dared not bring it up after that first morning on the porch.

He drove with furry, intensified by the alcohol, not really knowing why or what he would even say when he arrived, but he was now ready to deal with it, and she better dang well be ready too, he thought.

"Who tha hell she think she is hangin' up on me and then not gon' answer the phone?" The mumbles turned into a full-blown rant as thoughts raced through his mind the entire drive about how he would make her do what he needed her to do. Of course this meant doing what would be best for him.

He walked up to the entrance door and lay on the buzzer until she finally buzzed the door to let him in. She knew it was him. When he got to her apartment, he knocked loudly. Normally they were pretty quiet and discreet, but not this night, oh no, and Jim didn't care who heard.

She talked through the door. "Jim, what are you doing here?" she questioned.

"Open the door, Jane! What tha hell wrong with you? That baby got ya head all messed up." He was talking loudly.

Jane *shhh*'d him as she opened the door, and Jim burst in with raging flames bursting from the top of his head.

"Why did you hang up on me? Why didn't you answer the phone? You knew it was me calling," he yelled. The questions came back-to-back as he paced and waited for an answer.

Jane had never seen this side of Jim before. Sure, he could be sarcastic and a bit selfish, but he had never yelled at her in this way and acted so aggressively.

"Jim, stop yelling at me. You're scaring me." She backed away from him.

"Look, Jane, I done told you, I'm not playing this game with you." He walked across the room, snatching her by the arm. "You not having this baby."

She attempted to pull away, but his grip was tight. "Stop it. You're hurting me." Tears filled her eyes.

"Look what you makin' me do. I don't want to do this to you, Jane, but you ain't leaving me much choice." He sat on the couch, putting his head in his hands. "You just don't understand. Can't nothin' good come from this, and you know it. You always complaining about your life being hard being with me because I'm Black and because I'm married. How much harder you think it's about to get having this mixed-up baby?"

"That doesn't matter to me. Times are changing, Jim, and I'm not afraid. I wasn't afraid to be with you, and I'm not ashamed of being with you because you're Black. I'm ashamed because you're married, and I know it's not right, but I fell in love with you, Jim

Holloway. I didn't mean for it to happen. I don't really know what I thought I was doing, but I'm not apologizing for it."

"You really love me, Jane?" He stood and took her hand.

"You know I love you, don't you?" She pleaded with her eyes for him to understand the depths of her love.

"You just puttin' me in a bad position, Jane. A real bad position."

"Jim, please don't make me do this. I won't tell anyone whose baby it is. I promise."

"It ain't gonna be heard for people to figure it out, Jane. You not about to have no blond-haired, blue-eyed baby, and we both know that."

"My eyes are not blue." Rolling them, resenting the remark.

"I know they aren't blue Jane. You know exactly what I'm sayin'."

"You gotta just trust me. I'll protect you. I won't tell a soul, but I can't kill the life that's growing inside of me."

When he looked at Jane, he couldn't be angry. As much as he wanted to be, he just couldn't. She leaned over and kissed him softly, then passionately. It had been weeks since they had been intimate, and they both missed each other. Even though it was late, Jim didn't rush through it to get home that night. He made love to Jane as if he would never see her again. At almost 4 a.m., he gathered himself after she had fallen off to sleep and went home.

The Pregnancy

J ane had to talk to her mother about everything because she knew she couldn't do this alone. She had explained to Jim that her mother was the only person she would tell and that she would under no circumstances reveal it was him, but she had to tell her mother she was pregnant by a Black man because when the baby came, there would be no way of hiding it.

"Oh, Janie. Oh nooo. Oh Lord. How could you let this happen?" She walked back and forth the entire length of the kitchen. "And he's Black. See, this is what happens when you keep secrets. They always come out." Jane's mother knew she had been seeing someone the past couple of years and figured he had to be married because she never wanted to talk about it and never brought him around. If ever she asked about who Jane was dating and why they hadn't met him, she would just say it wasn't serious or make excuses about him not being available because of the type of work he did kept him on the road. It was always something, but never the truth. As much as she pried, Jane would never tell her much. Now when she decided to tell her it was an uncontrollable mess.

"I hope you don't think I'm telling your father. Oh nooo. That's going to be for you to do. This is horrid. Here I am thinking you're sneaking around with a married man, but it's much worse than that, now isn't it?" She leaned over onto the sink and took a deep breath. "Much, much worse."

Jane didn't have the heart to tell her he was married as well. Her mother might just pass out the way she was acting.

"This is going to kill your father. You know that don't you?" she turned and looked over at Jane. "It's simply going to kill him and it's going to be your fault that I am a widow."

Her mother, still in disbelief, began feverishly washing the dishes in the sink. She just needed to stay busy hoping it would calm her nerves. There were no further words uttered. All you could hear was the clinking of the dishes and the running of the water. Jane had no choice but to sit there for what seemed an eternity thinking about how stupid she felt. She knew she would need her parents' help, so she sat there and would sit until her mother decided how things would be handled. A while later, Jane's father's keys could be heard rustling at the back door.

"Hiya, sweetie. I saw your car outside." He leaned over and kissed her forehead. "How's my girl?"

"Pregnant," Jane's mom mumbled under her breath.

"Mom." Jane looked over at her.

"What's that, honey?" He walked over and kissed her on the lips.

"Nothing."

"Daddy," Jane said softly. She was so nervous. One thing she never wanted to do was disappoint her father. She never thought about any of this when she was feverishly plotting to make this child. Now, it seemed as if nothing was falling into place the way she hoped it would. She began to tell him what she had already divulged to her mother. He didn't take it as well as she did.

He jumped up from the table. "I'll kill him dead! Who is he? Who got my little girl knocked up? Did he hurt you? You know, did he force you to do this?"

"Gosh, Daddy. No."

"I'm calling your uncle. Give me this boy's address. We're going over there. He's not going to leave you holding the bag when you both were involved. He's going to marry you, don't you worry."

"No, Daddy. Calm down. It's not like that."

"Oh, just wait, there's more," Jane's mother blurted out.

"Well…" He looked at Jane waiting for a response. But she just sat there. She didn't want to tell him he was Black. When faced with her angry father, she blurted out…

"He's already married."

"What in the hell is wrong with you? You don't sleep with another woman's husband. You weren't raised like that." He walked over to the cabinet and got a glass, but his hand was shaking so he couldn't even fill the glass with water. "What are people going to say?"

"Is that all anyone cares about, what people are going to say? I don't care what they say. I love him."

"But he obviously doesn't love you because you're in my house telling me you're carrying a man's baby who isn't here standing by your side, but instead he's at his house with his wife and I'm guessing child or children. How could you be so naïve? Janie…"

Jane's mother took the glass and put it on the counter, went into the dining room, retrieved a shot glass and took a bottle of scotch from the cabinet. "Here you go. You're probably going to need this for what's coming next."

"Next? You mean there's more?" He leaned back in the chair and sipped the scotch. "I don't know how much more I can take."

"You hear that, Jane? Your dad doesn't think he can take anymore. What do you think?" At that point she decided to down a shot herself.

"He's Black, okay. There, I said it. The married man I've been having an affair with for over two years is a Black man! Happy, Mom?" She grabbed her purse and her keys and headed for the door.

"Wait, Jane." But Jane couldn't wait. She didn't think they'd react this way. She knew they wouldn't be proud, maybe even disappointed, but nothing like this.

"No. No. Let her go. She isn't bringing no half-breed baby in my house. I won't allow it. It's not right race mixing, and Civil Rights got these niggers thinking they can do what they want. See, I told you no good would ever come of giving them rights and letting them think they're something better than what they are. Now look. One of them went and tricked my baby girl. He probably raped her. There's no way she'd just let no colored get on top of her willingly. I didn't raise her like that. I just didn't. You best believe we're going to deal with his nigger ass too."

"Just calm down. She claims she loves him, and stop using that word. You know I don't like it."

"So you're okay with this?"

"No. I don't want her going around with a colored either, but that is what she chose."

"He probably threatened her or something. She don't love him. How could she? How's that even possible?"

"It's been over two years. It's something."

He poured another drink and threw the glass into the wall.

"I worked my whole life to give that girl everything she ever wanted, and this is how she repays me, getting herself knocked up by some darkie. Well, I'm not having it. I'm not. I'm not going to be the laughingstock of the lodge, the church and my whole damn neighborhood." He grabbed his keys and headed out the door.

No one would be able to understand what he was feeling. How could he face people? He just couldn't. He loved Jane, and he never thought of himself as being a racist. He just preferred things to stay the way they were. Why couldn't coloreds just be happy with what they had? We gave them a few rights, and now they think that entitles them to everything we have—everything we've worked for to make this nation the great land it is. *They're ruining everything. Everything,* he thought as he sat in his car in the driveway. He wanted to drive away, but where could he go to outdrive the situation? Where had he gone wrong? Girls were supposed to grow up and marry a man like their father, weren't they? He wasn't a very emotional man— passionate, but not emotional, but this six-foot, three-inch man sat in his car and wept like a baby.

Jane's mother watched through the window, knowing there was nothing she could say or do that would ease the embarrassment and pain his Jane had brought down on him that day. She knew she had to send Jane away. She went and got her phonebook out of her nightstand drawer and called her cousin. It was slightly uncomfortable to make the call, but Marilyn, her cousin, had grown up with her in Ohio and had moved away to New York when her husband got a job opportunity. But at one time, they were as close as sisters, but distance has a way of making you forget the people who are most important. She swallowed her pride and waited for someone to pick up on the other end.

"Hello," a cheery voice picked up.

"Marilyn."

"My word. Cindy, is that you?"

They both laughed like teenagers.

"Oh, it's so good to hear your voice. I miss you. To be quite honest, Marilyn, I really need your help."

"Well, of course, doll. What's the dilemma on your end?"

"Jane has gotten herself into a bit of a pickle, and it would be better for all involved if she could come stay with you for a bit."

"That kind of pickle?" Marilyn questioned sympathetically.

"I'm afraid so." She let out a sigh of exhaustion.

"Well, if you think it best, you send her right on. We'll take good care of her. You can rest assured."

After telling Marilyn the full story, they agreed to speak again once everything was worked out on their end.

She waited until later that night after dinner to bring it to Jane's father, which of course he agreed. At least that would give them time to come up with a story if nothing else, and he wouldn't have to face the ridicule he would undoubtedly experience if Jane stayed. They didn't want her to have an abortion, being the good churchgoing folk they were, but if she was willing to, they were all for it, no matter the risk or what the Christian belief said. It's always different when it's your situation. There's always room for the sin exception when it helps oneself, but after two conversations with her that week, they both realized she was keeping that baby no matter what type of logic they presented to her. Why she was trying to make her life hard, they couldn't understand. Things from this point were going to be different. No matter what rainbow, lollipop and gumdrop world she believed society was becoming, they weren't there that day, evidenced by her father's reaction. Adoption had even been given as an alternative, but again there was nothing anyone could say to convince Jane to part from her unborn child. So off to New York she went.

"I don't even have a backup," her father said softly.

"What?" Cindy asked.

"Nothing. It doesn't matter now."

"No. What did you say? Something about a backup? A backup what? Huh?"

"I said nothing okay. I'm sorry."

But she knew exactly what he meant: no backup child. In case one lets you down, you have a backup—a second chance to have one do you proud. But he was right, they had no backup. Cindy had such a hard time carrying Jane and then almost lost her and Jane's life during delivery, she was scared to even try to have more children. He had begged and promised her all would be fine, but it wasn't, and though he was by her side, he hadn't experienced what she had, and she decided one perfect child who was alive was better than two perfect children and a dead mother. He never really forgave her for it, but he learned to live with it.

According to Cindy and Marilyn, she would have the baby in New York and bring it back after the child's first birthday and act as if she was caring for her cousin's child who couldn't take care of her. She would be the saint cousin who was raising her cousin's illegitimate Black child. Upon her return, she would move to a new neighborhood where no one would know her to make the story more plausible. The plan sounded good—everyone would be covered—and Jane's parents could lie through their teeth to save their reputation. Most of all, Jim seemed to be okay with it all.

Since Jane would be leaving when she began to show, she and Jim spent as much time as they could together before she left. They packed all her things up and her dad and uncle moved most of it to her old bedroom. What wouldn't fit was stored in the attic and basement. Jim loved Jane, and though he still didn't want this baby, he would deal with it to appease her. After all, she had long since given up on having a normal family with a white picket fence when she decided to love Jim more than herself. However, she refused to give up being a mother. She believed every woman should have the right to be a mother—to experience creating, carrying and birthing life into this world if they so choose. She refused to forfeit that joy for Jim or anyone else.

Life was going according to plan. She had settled in to Cousin Marilyn's and was really loving the area and the doting her family was giving her, but when Jim wouldn't drive to New York to see her, all sorts of things went through her mind. She sat on the edge of the bed talking with her cousin Sarah, Marilyn's daughter, who simply couldn't understand how or why she had allowed herself to be trapped liked this. She really didn't care one way or the other about Jim being Black. Her big concern was the fact he was married and already had a family of his own with no intentions on ever leaving. Who would ask for a life like that?

"I just can't understand you, Jane. You've got so much going for you. You're pretty, you had your own place, your own job, and most of all nobody telling you when and where you can go or how much money you could spend. You were kinda independent, a real new woman." She came and sat next to her, and you're gonna give all that up for this man who can't even tell anybody this is his baby rolling around in your belly? He can't walk down the street and take y'all to the store and shop or go to Sunday breakfast. All you're thinking about is you, Jane. What about this baby? What kind of life are you setting it up for?"

"Be quiet, Sarah." Jane stood swiftly to her feet, pacing. "Don't you think I thought about that? Huh? Don't you?" She raised her voice frantically as she drowned in her cousin's words. Her agitation showed as she bolted from the bed and paced in a circle.

"Well hell, Jane, I don't know. I don't know what's going on in that nutty head of yours. I know you weren't thinking about this baby basically growing up and being taught to lie and be ashamed of who his daddy is and how his whore mother was screwing somebody else's husband."

Jane walked right over and slapped Sarah with all her might. Sarah grabbed her face.

"You mad, Janie? You're mad at the wrong person. The person you should be mad at is you. That's who your baby is going to be mad at: you! You gonna slap it, too, when it tells you the truth?"

Sarah walked over to the mirror to inspect the damage to find Jane's red handprint across her face. "If you weren't pregnant, I would kick your ass, Jane. Really I would."

"Language," Jane said snidely.

"Language?" Sarah threw her head back. "Ha! Now that's rich coming from my unwed pregnant cousin. You wish language was your biggest worry." She chuckled. "I can stop cursing, but you can't stop being pregnant."

Jane sunk to the floor in tears. She knew Sarah was right, but she didn't want to hear it.

"Sarah, I'm sorry. I–I just…" she stuttered. "I don't know, I just thought it was going to be different once I got pregnant."

"Did you do this on purpose?" Sarah questioned her with a disapproving voice of amazed disbelief. Jane's silence told her all she needed to know. "How could you be so stupid? I really used to look up to you. I always wished I was as brave as you, but I had no idea bravery led to stupidity."

"I don't know, I just thought once I told him you know, once he knew I was carrying his baby he would just go ahead and leave so we could be a family."

She fell back looking at a small baby spider crawling across the ceiling. She wondered where it was off to, wished she could escape with it, but fully knew it would meet a fate of complete and utter destruction once someone saw it and smashed it. It was at that moment she realized she was now a bug—a bug waiting to be squashed. Squashed by a society that would never understand her situation. Squashed by raising a child alone. Squashed by disapproving whispers and squashed by the words of those who claimed to love her but simply could never understand how she of all people wound up in this situation.

"It's not like they even have a real marriage. He doesn't even love her."

"It doesn't matter, Janie. Don't you get it? He loved her enough to marry her, and he loves her enough to not leave her to be with you. Besides, don't they have children? I mean didn't she carry his babies, too, and what did that get her, a lying, cheating husband? I know it's different with you, right? It's always different with the mistress. You get to be all fun all the time, and now you've messed up that fun, so don't be surprised if he cheats on you with somebody with no kids so he can have more fun. I know that may hurt, but it's just the truth. You didn't have any business messin' around with that lady's husband, no way around it. You are wrong, and no one is going to feel sorry for you. It's just the plain-and-simple truth, and you might as well get used to it and decide what you gonna do next. Maybe you should just stay here where nobody knows you. You could start all over."

But Jane couldn't do this. Her life was in Ohio. Her love was in Ohio, and she wasn't giving him up no matter what people said or thought. Not even him.

Month eight of that pregnancy, she just couldn't take it anymore. She needed to see Jim. It had been three very long months, and she broke. She knew she was supposed to stay there and have the baby, but she wanted to be near Jim. She needed to see his face, feel the caress of his hand on her cheek. Against her husband's wishes, Sarah drove over to her mother's, which was where Jane was staying, packed her up into the car and headed for an adventure. This was undoubtedly the bravest thing Sarah had ever done. She not only defied her husband's wishes, her mother and father's wishes, but she was going to drive seven hours in doing so. She and Tom had been married nearly six years but had not been able to have children as of yet, but it wasn't for a lack of trying. Tom could be a little possessive and controlling so this was big for her. She secretly hoped it would give her a foot into a little more freedom. She never really stood up to him before as she did that day. She would always cower down and end of up doing whatever he thought was best even when she didn't even close to agree.

Don't understand wrong. He was a great guy, but while he lived life on his own terms, Sarah was also stuck living her life by those same terms whether she liked it or not. They were high school sweethearts, and well, when a man that you loved asked you to marry them, you say yes so you didn't wind up old and alone. You pop out a few kids and have a great life. No one prepares you for the possibility of the perfect plan having a life of its own and making its own changes.

Sarah tossed Jane's suitcase into the backseat as she waddled to the car and her heart filled with excitement. She closed the door after Jane got in, hurried around, got in on the driver's side and closed the door.

"Are you sure about this?" Sarah asked as she handed the map off to Jane.

"Yep."

"Okay, here we go. My first real adventure and just another for the books for you." They both laughed.

"Thanks, Sarah."

"Hey, that's what cousins who only saw each other once a year growing up do for each other, right? I know I have been hard on you, but it's just preparing you because the world is going to be that much harder. But I love you and still admire your blind boldness." She chuckled and shook her head, and they hit the road.

When they arrived at her parents', she knew they would be upset, but they told her she had to go back to New York. She couldn't stay there.

"Did anyone see you?" her mother scoffed.

"I can't believe that's all you're worried about. Well, great to see you, too, Mother."

"I'm just glad your father isn't here, and Sarah, I can't believe you allowed her to manipulate you into this nonsense of a life she's hell bent on destroying." She went straight to the kitchen and began clanking pots and pans mumbling about them being hungry and both being foolish and what was she expecting coming back here. Jane didn't know what was worse, the clanking or the discouraging venom spewing from her mouth.

That night she knew exactly where Jim would be, and pregnant and all, she went to the club. She waited in the car and sent Sarah in the club. Jane had shown her a picture of Jane and Jim taken with a Polaroid. She waited anxiously in the car. Sarah was very apprehensive as she made her way in and looked around for Jim. She felt uncomfortable as people stared at her. She finally spotted him toward the front sitting with a few people, talking and laughing. The laughter paused as she walked up.

"Well, what do we have here?" one of the guys at the table eyeballed her as she approached. They all laughed.

"What you do, Jim? Get you a stand-in while Jane is gone?" He slapped Jim's back.

"I just might have ta if she lookin' to be. Are you lookin' Milky White?" Jim said to Sarah.

"Ummm." Sarah cleared her throat nervously stuttering.

"Well, are ya?" Jim questioned.

"*Ummm,* no. *Ummm,* I'm Jane's cousin. *Umm,* she's outside in the car and asked me to come find you." Her words were shaky as she wrung her hands and moved from side to side.

"*Awww,* sh—" his friend Charlie said.

"What's she doin' outside in the car? Why she ain't in New York?"

"She said she needed you, and I brought her."

"You drove her here?"

"I did."

"By yaself?"

"Yes." She wondered why all the questions.

"Well then you just as stupid as her right about now."

"Yes. That's what I keep hearing." She shook her head and repeated, "That's what I keep hearing" in a defeated voice.

They made their way toward the door.

"Where is she?"

Sarah led him to the car. As soon as she saw Jim, she jumped out the car hugged him and began to kiss him and cry.

"What are you doing here?" He pulled her arms from around his neck, forcing her back into the car and getting in after her.

"I thought you were going to stay in New York until the baby came."

"Well, you wouldn't come to see me. I just couldn't be away from you any longer, Jim baby. I just couldn't. I'm dying, and I feel alone without you. I need you. Your baby needs you."

"Look, we done been through this a thousand times. I can't make it no plainer. I didn't want this baby, but ain't nothing I can do it about it now, but you can't force me to play daddy. I already got kids, and I'm gonna be there for y'all, but you askin' me for somethin' I just ain't got in me, Jane. Now I love you, but you making me feel trapped."

"You feel trapped. What about me, Jim? What about me? I'm the one carrying this baby and gotta be there for this baby no matter what. You ain't trapped. You doin' what Jim always does. What's best for Jim." She rolled down the window. "Sarah, let's go. This was a mistake." She looked at Jim. "You ain't who I thought you were, Jim Holloway." She had never looked at him that way before, and he didn't like it. It was the same feeling he had when Lizzie said she didn't want to have anything else to do with him and she had killed their baby. The one baby he wanted.

"Jane."

"It's alright, Jim. I'll be fine—no, we'll be fine. If you don't want my baby, you don't want me. I can't believe I wasted all these years on you—gave up any hopes and dreams I had for myself if they couldn't include you. But that's alright. You want me gone, you want us gone, we're gone."

"Jane, wait. No."

"I've been waiting a long time, Jim, for nothing. I can't wait anymore. I can't live for you anymore. I can't, and I won't. Get out the car, Jim, please. I don't want to look at you right now. You broke my heart like I never thought you could."

He didn't resist. He didn't try to comfort her with words. He just slunk out of the car and let her ride off and thought that was for the best. He missed her something terrible, which just made things worse for Josephine and the girls. He went back into the club and had a few more drinks.

"So what was that about?" Bobby asked.

"I still don't know, Bobby. She said she missed me and had to see me but just 'cause I won't be who she needs me to be. I think she just told me she don't want me no more." He tossed back another drink.

"Woah, man, I think you done had your fill tonight. Let me take you home."

"*Hmmm.* She don't want me unless I want her and that bastard baby she 'bout to have," he slurred. "She know who she dealin' with?" He took his right arm and pounded his fist into his chest. "I'm Jim Holloway. I don't need her. She needs me. She's the one who drove from New York to get to me, right, Bobby?"

"Right, Jim. You right."

"You need to get him on outta here," Charlie said.

Jim knocked off one more drink as they stumbled to Bobby's car.

All he talked about on the way to the house was Jane. It was painful to hear. How could he allow himself to get in this mess? Bobby was never going to understand it. Shoot, nobody could. When they pulled up to the house, all the lights were out. Bobby fumbled around with Jim trying to get his house key. He almost hated to leave him there because he just didn't know what state of mind he was in. Jim hardly ever let you know what he was really feeling. I guess if you don't allow yourself to feel you can't get hurt. Bobby told Jim to just stay down on the couch and sleep it off. When Josephine heard the whispering and bumbling commotion, she put her robe on and came downstairs.

"Uh, hey, Josephine. I'm sorry we woke you. Jim had a few too many, and I didn't want him trying to drive. You know."

"Oh, I understand, Bobby. You're a good friend. Thank you. I'll take it from here."

"Y'all gonna be alright?"

"Yeah. Go on now." She went upstairs and got a blanket to lay over him. Just as she was covering him up, he grabbed her wrist. "Hey, Josephine, do you love me?"

"Of course I love you, Jim. I always have. Why you askin' a question like that?"

"Come here." He began pulling at her pajamas. "Come show me."

"Jim, you're just drunk. Go on now." She turned to walk away.

"I said come show me." He grabbed her.

"Jim, please don't do this. What if one of the children come down the stairs?"

"They're sleep. Now come on here, Jo." He pulled her down to her knees and got behind her. "See, this ain't so bad right." He laughed. "This yo' job, girl. "Gon' tell me she don't want me. Plenty people want me. Ain't that right, Jo? You want me, don't you?"

When he finished, she got up and went to the shower. It wasn't rough or forced, but there was no love there. It was empty. She felt like a waste receptacle. What had happened to the man she had fallen so in love with? How did he become this thing? Some days were surely unbearable. Times like this, she would rather him just slap her one good time so she could be on her way. She hated to feel him inside her. She flinched when he touched her. The same hands that once caused her body to melt and yearn for more touches had become a nightmare. Jim was so into himself. He never even bothered to care if she was responsive during sex. It was only about his needs being met in their house. It was different with Jane though, much different.

Josephine knew something was going on because he had needs frequently the last several months. She just figured he and Jane were on the outs. Of course she knew about Jane. She was no fool, but at this point in her life, she didn't even care. Whatever kept him away was heaven-sent in her mind. He of course didn't know she knew at that point, and what would be the point of telling him? It's not like it would straighten him out by any means.

Jane went back to New York, her heart broken in pieces and her pride more damaged than she could have imagined, especially in front of Sarah. This was not at all how this had played out in her mind on the drive there. She had truly believed Jim would see her and realize how he had missed her and take her in her arms, kiss her and profess how much he had missed her. What a sorry state she had found herself in. She began to regret getting pregnant, but now this life was growing inside her, there was no way she would even consider terminating the pregnancy. Adoption was always an option, but she could never bring herself to give away her child either. She realized at that very moment how much harder she had made her life. She wept practically the whole drive back to New York. Her head pressed against the window pondering what she'd do next.

They had left first thing the next morning for New York, which made her parents very happy. They secretly hoped all this would fall apart. They hated Jim and how he had stolen their daughter's life. Jim, on the other hand, didn't see it that way. She went looking for something, and she found it. It wasn't Jim's fault it was him she had found.

When Jim woke up that morning, his head ached from back to front and side to side, and his stomach was in knots. He made his way to the kitchen and drank some Alka-Seltzer. He felt like garbage, not just physically, but emotionally. Why did he do that to Jane? Why couldn't he have just been happy to see her and dealt with the baby stuff later? He didn't know why he was the way he was, and even when he thought about being somebody different, he couldn't.

Weeks had gone by, and he decided to call Jane up at her aunt's. Her aunt reluctantly allowed Jane to speak with him. He just needed to know how she was doing, but more than anything, he wanted to hear her voice. He wanted to know he still had her, that she still belonged to him. He wasn't really sure the way she had left, but he wasn't about to show his weakness just because she drove from Timbuktu to see him.

"Jim, what do you want?"

"Now, why you talkin' like that?"

"You made it clear you didn't want me there, and you don't even want your own flesh and blood, so why are you calling me? Isn't it easier for you having me out the picture? Now you can run on and get you another girl who's not pregnant, and you can go back to your double life."

He stood on the other end of that phone wanting to hang up, wanting to curse her, but he didn't. He took the phone in his hand, raised it over his head and took a humiliating deep breath before responding.
"It's not like that, and you know it."

"Well, what is it like, Jim? Huh? Tell me what it's like. Maybe I got it all wrong." The sarcasm in her voice was thick.

"Listen, Jane, I don't need the BS right now. I just wanted to see how you were feeling. I know it's getting close to time for the baby, and I guess…" He paused. "I guess I just wanna know you're alright."

"And again I ask, you care because…?" There was a long pause before Jim hung up. He mumbled to himself. "I ain't gotta deal with this. Man, who she think she is?"

Jane immediately regretted her response to the call, but she was tired. The baby coming was beginning to change her perspective about a lot of things. She wanted Jim, but now, her and the baby were a package, simple as that. But maybe she shouldn't have been so hard on him. She just didn't know what to do. Jim was never going to be what she needed him to be to her, and it hurt.

After the baby came, she waited two months before going back to Ohio—a year was just too long. Her parents reluctantly allowed her to come home and stay with them while she looked for a new job. As much as she loved having her parents' help, her mother was smothering. She needed her space, and deep down inside she wanted to be able to see Jim, and she knew they would never allow it.

Jane had called Jim's house a few times but hung up because it was never him who answered. She attempted finding him in the local clubs and bars. She called his Friday night hangout and asked the bartender if he was there. He was. He called Jim to the phone. He thought it was probably Josephine and figured something must be wrong.

He grabbed the phone from Ray, the bartender. "This Jim."

"Hey, Jim. It's Jane. I was just letting you know you have a son. He's beautiful too."

The call caught him off guard. He didn't really know how to respond. "Oh, *ummm,* that's good. You do alright with the labor and all?"

"Yes, I did."

They both just held the phone, not really knowing what to say. Where were they now? Things could never go back to the way they were, and they both knew this.

"Well, I'm glad you okay." He broke the silence.

"Did you wanna see him, Jim?"

"Uh yeah…yeah…I guess." He choked. "I mean of course I wanna see him." He paused and took a breath. "And I wanna see you, too, Jane—that is if you want to see me."

Butterflies filled her stomach. She couldn't let on. She played down her emotions, but was glad he said he wanted to see her.

"Sure. Sure, Jim, that would be fine. I don't think my parents will be okay with you coming here, so I guess we can meet somewhere or I can see if Tiffany will let us come to her house."

"I'll just get a motel room, and you can come there. I don't need all eyes gawkin' at me, judgin' me. I just ain't puttin' myself through that."

"Well alright, Jim. I understand."

They set up the date and time three days out. Jane was a little nervous. She parked around back and waited until she saw Jim's car pull in. After getting the key, she watched which door he went in and shortly thereafter she and their new baby, Michael, went in. She made her best effort not to be needy. She spoke, kissed Jim on the cheek and began to unwrap the blanket Michael was in.

Jim waited patiently, but did wonder why the kiss was on the cheek instead of the mouth. He didn't say anything, but it did cross his mind. Maybe she was upset with him for hanging up or simply not being there, but whatever the case, he could tell she was different.

"Well, here he is. Do you want to hold him?" Jim held out his arms. "Oh, he's so little. Hey, little man. Hey. Do you know who I am? I'm your father. That's right. I'm your father."

Jane got excited when she heard those words and saw how Jim held him and talked to him. Shortly after arriving, she nursed him, and he fell right on to sleep. She laid him down on the bed, then turned to Jim with the intention of laying down some ground rules of him being in or out of their lives, but as soon as she turned around, she turned right into him. He was standing over her shoulder looking at little Michael. As soon as she turned, he kissed her, and she didn't resist.

"You did good, Jane. You really did, especially by yourself. I'm sorry I couldn't be there, and if things were different, I would have been, but they're just not, and I can't change that." He took her face in his hands and kissed her again. "I'll try to be here as best I can, but I can't make no promises, and you can't be getting all mad and crazy when I can't be, you hear? Come on now, get out them clothes before the baby wakes up."

"Are you serious? No, no, Jim. I didn't come here to have sex. Is that what this was about?"

"Wait. What? Do you think I just had you come here to screw? I can do that anytime. I just missed you is all, and the way you just kissed me, I thought that's what you wanted. We ain't gotta have sex. I thought that's what you wanted. I just can't win with you, girl." He grabbed his jacket and headed for the door.

"So you leaving 'cause I won't have sex with you?"

"No, I'm leaving because I don't know what you want, Jane. I'm here, and I'm trying, but I'm not succeeding, and I like to be a success at everything I do. If I can't succeed at something, that means it ain't my thing. Maybe this ain't my thing. I don't know what I was thinking comin' here. I don't know what I expected, but I didn't expect to get rejected by you of all people."

"Jim, wait. Don't leave. You gotta understand it from my side. You left me. You left me to do it all by myself. You didn't want Michael. I had to track you down, not the other way around, and you show up, hold your child ten minutes, and think I wanna have sex." The tears began to flood her eyes. She tried to stop them, but she couldn't.

"Here we go. I don't need all this. I just want things back the way they were. Man. You messed up everything. Look what's happening to us. Just look." He sat in the chair with his head in his hands in frustration. "What do you want, Jane?"

"What I want you're incapable of giving, not just to me, but probably to anyone. I never realized it until this very moment. I've been living in a fantasy world to ever think we could be together. You had my mind all mixed up, Jim, but the baby helps me think clear because my whole world was Jim, and now you can't come first anymore. Hell, I can't come first anymore, and it's hard, and it hurts because all I know is this—is you."

"When are you moving out?"

"Wait. What?"

"When are you movin'? I can't be a part of his life or yours if you're livin' at your parents' house."

"Now you want to be a part of Michael's life? I don't understand you, Jim. You can't keep going back and forth. You want us, you don't. Which is it because I don't have any more years to waste? I have to start thinking about a real future for me and my son."

"I know, Janie. I know. I'm trying here, okay? I'll help you, but you gotta move or you know it will be like this all the time— meeting in motel rooms. He's gonna start gettin' older and then what?"

Jane was hesitant initially, but no matter what she spewed out of her mouth, she was in love with Jim, no ifs, ands, whats or buts. And it wasn't long before Jane had found a job and her mother was taking care of Michael during the day. Jim helped Jane financially, and she and Michael wanted for nothing. Her father had still not warmed up to the idea that Michael was fathered by a Black man, so he didn't spend much time trying to love him or know him. Initially, he was against Cindy keeping the baby during the day.

"What are the neighbors going to think? You walking 'round here with this half-breed baby. It makes no sense, Cindy, and I'm not having it."

"You can't stop me from helping my child and loving my grandchild. It's not his fault. and I'm gonna love him just the same as if he were White, and if you have a problem with it, it's your problem, not mine."

That was that. Time moved forward, and in Jane's mind, she, Jim and Michael were a family. She never let the fact that he already had a family deter her reality. When Jim was with them, it was as if they didn't exist, and that's what she made herself believe. As awful as it was, it's how she lived with it.

But again, enough about Jim and Jane, let's get back to the funeral.

Back to the Funeral

Diane caught up to the mysterious woman at the back of the church just as she was rounding the corner to exit.

"Hey. Excuse me." She tapped Jane on the shoulder. "I don't mean to be rude, but how do you know my dad?"

Jane stood there for a moment deciding how to answer. Did she tell her who she was, that this was her little brother, that Jim was the love of her life, or did she simply say just a friend and walk away?

"*Ummm,* are you okay? Diane questioned.

"I am Jane," she managed to get out.

"Okay, and how did you know my dad?"

"This really isn't the time or place for that discussion. I'm sorry." She turned to walk away.

"Now's as good a time as any." She followed her. Michael grabbed Jane's hand tightly. "I wanna go, Mommy," he said timidly.

"Hi. I'm sorry. Did I frighten you?" She squatted down eye level to Michael. "If I did, I didn't mean to. My name is Diane." She stuck her hand out and shook his hand. "Nice to meet you."

He stuck his hand out and smiled. "Nice to meet you too. Are you mad my daddy is gone too?"

"I was real sad, and then I was mad, and now I'm sad again."

"My mommy has been really sad for a lot of days."

"That's enough, Michael. Let's go." She attempted to scurry him along as her face grew flush and dizziness came upon her.

"Nice to meet you, Michael. I'm sorry you lost your dad." Then she called out to Jane, "You did know he was married, didn't you, and that my mother is an amazing woman who dealt with his bullshit for far too long? You know that, right?"

She threw the nice-nasty words at her.

She walked back into the church, deciding if it was even worth mentioning. So torn, she thought it best to leave it be. She knew it was wrong, but she was glad he was gone. He made their lives miserable. They had no tears to shed, unless she counted tears of joy. They couldn't experience the apparent sadness Jane was plagued by. Why was she so sad? Who was Jim to her? Yes, they had a son, but what did that mean? The confusion was overwhelming. They genuinely appeared grief stricken. What kind of life was he over there offering up, and why were they not good enough for it?

That night, Jane sat on her bed doing all she could not to cry. Michael was asleep in her bed, where he had chosen to be since her sadness had come upon her. She reflected on her life with Jim and the obstacles they had overcome to get to where they were, only for him to be snatched away. She knew in her heart of hearts that Jim was eventually going to leave Josephine. He was spending more and more time with her and their son. She just felt it was coming. Life was unfair. She called her best friend who was not as sympathetic as she had hoped. Her take was more or less oh well, it was karma. She had no business hoping a man would leave his wife to be with her. She told her it was wrong from the beginning, and therefore could only end wrong. There was no way to dress it up. In life, you can't always get what you want just because you want it. Jane didn't understand that. She wanted someone to be on her side, to understand what she was experiencing. She was supposed to be her friend and just love her unconditionally and be there for her when she needed her. That's what a real friend did, and that was her expectation, which was not quite met. The only person she had sympathy for was Michael who was the innocent child in this whole situation.

After ending the phone call with her unsympathetic friend, she paced in the living room drinking a glass of wine. She pictured Jim rolling around on the living room floor last Christmas with Michael and thought how he would never have that experience with his dad again.

Jim had started that Christmas Day at home. They had all gotten up early as they did every year. Josephine had made a huge breakfast consisting of coffee cake, fried as well as scrambled eggs, grits, sausage, fresh fruit and Honey's favorite, the lightest, fluffiest pancakes with fresh whipped cream and bananas. It's not that Honey was her favorite, but she was her baby girl—the last one she would have—and she held on to her dearly.

The kids were older at that point, so there was no rush to the tree. There was excitement in the air just because it was Christmas. They had decided to skip Christmas morning service because the weather was so bad. This was one of the days where all was right. Everyone was happy. There was laughter and jokes as they sat around the table. Even Jim was at ease and seemed to be enjoying his family. These moments were not frequent, but as bad as Jim was, when he was good, he was a different person. This rare glimpse was not seen often enough, but the girls always seemed to let their guard down when Dad showed up instead of Jim. When there was a small lull in the conversation and laughter, Jim got up from the table and came back with wrapped boxes and began to play Santa, handing gifts to each of the girls and Jim Jr.

"Girls, I hope you all like what I picked out for you. I wasn't really sure, but I had been trying to listen to hear what you girls had been talking about lately, and I did my best."

Honey leaned over her box and wondered why she couldn't always have a father. She opened the beautifully wrapped box, and tears flooded her eyes. It was the coat she was telling Diane she had seen and wanted from May Company.

"It's perfect, Daddy. Just perfect."

She wanted to go hug him, but was still quite reserved and hesitant, so she just stood and tried it on and modeled it around as he pulled another box from the floor.

"Well, here. You'll need these too." She tore into the box to witness the baddest pair of boots she could imagine. "The lady at the department store said these were the boots all the girls wanted right now. I hope she was right."

"She was right," Diane said. "Whew, Honey, you're gonna knock 'em dead when you step out the house." She fanned herself with her hand. They all laughed.

Each of them received their gifts and were all happy to have them.

"This was nice, Jim. This was real nice," Josephine said.

"Oh, I didn't forget you now, Jo." He went out to the garage again before returning with four boxes. There was a coat, new shoes, a new pocketbook and a new dress. "Jo—" He walked over to her and motioned for her to stand— "I know I ain't all I should be, but…" He paused. "I'm all I can be." He reached in his pocket and pulled out a small box and handed it to her. She slowly opened it to find a beautiful sapphire necklace.

"Oh," she gasped. "It's beautiful, Jim. It's just beautiful."

"Here, turn around and let me put it on you."

Josephine turned and met eyes with Diane. They both wondered through their expressions what this was all about. They dared not question it though. They thought they had better sit back and enjoy it while it lasted. They gave one another a smile of agreement. As she turned back toward him, he kissed her on the cheek.

"Beautiful. It looks real nice on you, Jo. Real nice." He seemed to be lost in his thought. He was remembering how beautiful she was when he first met her—how much life she once had—and he knew he was the reason she was the shell of who she once was. This instantly angered him. He quickly sat down at the table. "June, get me some coffee." He suddenly seemed bothered and slightly agitated.

June returned with the coffee, and he stirred in a small amount of milk. As he stared at the milk slowly being enveloped by the blackness of the coffee, it made him think of Jane. He had done the exact same thing to Jane. He had taken her over. He couldn't help it.

It's just what he did. They finished up breakfast, and Josephine and Diane began clearing the dishes away. The next thing they knew, Jim had his coat on and was headed for the door.

"I need to take care of some things. I'll be back in a bit."

The weather was so bad and Josephine wanted to know where he was going on Christmas Day. Her face spoke how badly she wanted to question him, but the morning had been so nice, and she didn't want to ruin it by setting him off. She gave a nod of sadness as she continued to clean.

June looked at Josephine with pity. "Momma, don't be fooled by that show this morning. He's still just Jim. You deserve better. You deserve better, Momma."

"Shoot. What you are you talking about, girl? If it wasn't for him, I wouldn't have all of you. You girls are the best part of him. Hopefully Jim Jr. will stop trying so hard to be like his dad. You girls may never understand, but I understand Jim, and though I don't like what I have come to understand, I do understand. He's in a lot of pain, but I don't know why. Child, it's deep inside of him, and he's slowly allowing it to eat away at him, and sometimes when he just can't take no more, he lets it out, and I'm the closest thing to him, so he lets it out on me a lot of times. It's not right, but it's Jim. Now I'm not making excuses, and I'm not sayin' it's right. It's just what it is, and I have to keep a roof over y'all heads. It's not like I can get out here and take care of all of us by myself. Your father is a good provider, and he works hard to give us things most Black folks only dream about. I hope you never have to understand what I mean."

She turned toward the sink in an attempt to hold the tears back. She had dreams once, and when she met Jim, she was content with the dream of building a life with him and making a family and being in love and growing old and watching grandchildren grow and laugh and play when visiting. Life snatched every last dream and replaced it with seasons of happiness, seasons of pain and many days of numbness. Her children were what she lived for, and she wouldn't trade them for the world.

Jim traveled through the storm to get to his other family, arriving at Jane's house with gifts for Michael and for Jane, but she was used to getting things from Jim all year round, so it wasn't a big production. He somehow thought the gifts could make up for the situation being what it was. For these few hours on Christmas Day, Jane got the family she wanted. They were miles and miles away from reality, where she could create the life she envisioned, even if only for a day.

Jim struggled initially with Michael, but he was sweet and lovable and wanted nothing more than to be with his daddy every chance he could. His smile softened Jim in a way he didn't know was possible since Lizzie had broken his heart many years ago. He and Jane never hid their affection in front of Michael, and as far as he knew, they were a family. It wasn't until he started kindergarten that he began to ask the hard questions, like why his dad never came to his school like some of the other kids and why his daddy didn't live with him. These questions would break Jane's heart and irritate Jim when she would dig into him about them.

Some of the teachers whispered about her, and one parent expressed she did not want her son in the same class with this mixed child. No one knew for certain, but they all speculated his father had to be Black, and it made things that much harder for him as well as added unwanted strain on Jane and Jim's relationship.

Jane would give anything to argue with him right now. She longed to beg him not to leave, to grab hold to him and tell him she loved him. She wished she could watch him hover in the doorway of Michael's bedroom watching him sleep before leaving for the night as he often did. It was so unfair. She cried even more and sank down onto the floor. The cries turned into desperation for answers and direction. What would she do without Jim? He wasn't perfect, but she loved him with a sincere almost uncontrollable love. It was wrong, but it worked for them, and she didn't care what anyone else thought.

That same night across town, Josephine cried silent tears as she lay in the empty bed. The funeral made it so final. Her heart broke for the man he never allowed himself to be. She cried out to God, wondering what was next. What was she supposed to do now? She had forgotten what it was like to breathe and to think without wondering how Jim would react. She sat up on the side of the bed before grabbing her robe and going downstairs. She was surprised to see Jim's mother sitting at the kitchen table drinking a cup of tea.

"Couldn't sleep either?" she said to Josephine.

"Not really. Feels scary and sad—" she sighed— "and lonely and different and freeing all at the same time."

Ruth wanted to know what had really been going on because no one in that house mourned the way you would think a family who has lost their husband and father would.

Before long, Diane came down for water. "Oh, can I crash the party? You okay, Momma?"

"How can she be okay? Her husband was killed! And why…why would you use the word *party*? This is not a celebration. My son is dead," she exclaimed. "Dead. How could this happen?" She broke down in tears.

Diane stood back fighting to be respectful. "This could happen to anyone but even more so to a man who made my mother's life a living hell. He was a mean bastard who robbed my mother of her life, and no matter how terrible he was, she always stood by him and always made excuses for him." Diane's voice got louder and louder before she calmed herself and mumbled, "Tired, sorry self." She leaned on the wall and exclaimed, "So forgive me if my grief or lack thereof isn't acceptable to you. It's obvious you no longer knew your dead son." She turned and walked out the kitchen.

Ruth looked at Josephine somewhat embarrassed as she got up and left the kitchen. She didn't know what to say. She knew Diane wouldn't just make these things up, and Josephine didn't stop her.

Jim Jr. had been in the living room sitting in his father's chair. He jumped up and caught Diane by her arm. "What's wrong with you? Why would you tell her that?"

"Because it's the truth. Her son was no angel, and she gonna come here and try to judge us—judge our feelings not knowing anything about us."

"You're a real bitch, Diane."

They continued to argue until Jim Jr. slapped Diane straight across her face and told her to shut up. She was stunned, but once she realized what had happened, she jumped on his back as he was walking away. They fell onto the coffee table knocking the *Time* and *Ebony* magazines to the floor and breaking the candy dish. The noise and wrestling woke everyone up. Josephine was attempting to pull Jim off Diane when June walked in.

"What is going on?"

She saw Josephine fall back into the wall as Jim pushed her off him. He and Diane continued to fight, rolling on the floor until Jim Jr. began choking her. Honey ran in and jumped on his back, and before you knew it all three girls were trying to hold him down. Diane's lip and nose were busted.

"Lord, help me. Like father, like son. You gonna beat your own sister. Is that the one thing you gonna take from your father? Jesus. Jesus. Jesus. I can't take it. I just can't take it. Everybody go to their rooms—now. June, fix Diane up. Jim Jr., I'll tell you this, if you ever put your hands on anyone in this house again, I love you, but I swear I will put you out of here. Do you hear me? Jim's spirit is not gonna live in this house through you. Do you hear me?"

They were all shocked. She had never stood up for herself, and Jim would never let her really discipline Jim Jr., so it was all too much to take in.

Honey went right in the room with June and Diane to find out what happened. They were proud of Josephine. They joked it was worth the fight to bring that out of her. They laid back on the bed and laughed.

"Ouch! My face hurts. I can't laugh," Diane whispered.

This threw them into another fit of laughter. They realized they were now free to all stay in June's room that night, and they did.

The next day was new, fresh and unfamiliar, but it was welcomed. The goodbye with Jim's family was awkward and empathetic. Ruth had no idea what Josephine had endured at the hands of Jim, but she had come out on top. They all hugged each child one by one in an almost apologetic way, even Jim Jr. after his behavior the previous night. When Ruth got to Josephine, she held her tightly.

"I am so, so sorry. If you need anything, please let me know." She kissed her on the cheek and squeezed her arms, affirming her concern. "I love you," she whispered. "I would still like the chance to get to know you and the children, if you think it would be alright." She looked heartbroken, but for so many reasons, it was hard to pinpoint which emotion was manifesting in the moment.

"I would like that." Josephine hugged her once more, and they both smiled. In an instant, they were in the car and headed down the street, as if they had never been there at all.

The Will

J osephine had to call Carl to find out what she needed to do about Jim's life insurance. They both had life insurance, but she hadn't seen the policies since they had signed them years ago. Carl informed her he had already filed the necessary paperwork, and he had planned on calling her to set the appointment to read the will, but she beat him to it. She didn't understand all the formalities, She thought she would just sign the insurance papers and that would be that.

"Appointment for a will reading? Is that really necessary?" she questioned Carl.

He assured her it was as Jim left a will and she wasn't the only beneficiary.

The day she entered Carl's office and was instructed to sit in the conference room and wait, she couldn't be prepared for what was to unfold. She and the children were there as well as Jane and Michael. When June and Diane saw Jane sitting there, though they were in shock, they were not at all surprised. Josephine kept her composure as she looked over at Jane. She knew exactly who she was, but nothing could have prepared her for Michael. She knew Jim was lowdown, but she never imagined he had sunk that low. It all came back to her: the woman walking around the casket holding the little boy's hand. She had never seen Jane before, but undoubtedly with this White woman being here for the reading of the will, which

Josephine didn't even know Jim had, was a clear indication she was in fact Jane.

Jim Jr. came in and saw her. "Hello, Miss Jane."

She looked up. "Jim Jr." She smiled at him, almost thanking him for acknowledging her.

Diane cut her eyes at Jim Jr. "You always were a traitor. You're sorry just like your sorry daddy."

"That's enough." Josephine interrupted what was getting ready to turn into something out of control.

Carl came in and kissed Josephine on the cheek. "I am so sorry I have do to this in this manner, but I have to follow Jim's wishes. I would never intentionally hurt you or disrespect you, Josephine."

He was sincere, and she didn't hold Jim's nonsense against him. He looked over at Jane with disgust, however, he did smile at Michael. "Good morning, young man."

"Good morning, sir," Michael managed to nervously get out.

"Well, let's get started," he said as he took a seat at the head of the table in the conference room and opened his briefcase. He began by stating the reason they all knew they were there and then commenced to handing each of them an envelope containing a letter written by Jim. "You all were only to receive these letters in the event of Jim's death. They were each written at different times over the last three years. Honey, I'm sorry to say there isn't one for you, and Jane, there isn't one for Michael. Each letter has a date so you'll know when it was written, but I haven't myself read them. Now, I'm supposed to read this, written by Jim:

'If you're hearing these words, it's because I've gone on to a better place as the old folks used to say. At least I hope I have. I know I ain't been the best man I could have been, but I was only what I could be. Life is hard, and fighting your demons every day gets the better of you some days, so each of you should have a letter telling you what I need you to know.'"

Carl cleared his throat, "Now for the reading of the will:

"'Josephine, of course you will keep the house for you and the kids, and the life insurance is enough to pay it in full and leave you some extra money to maybe do something you really want to do. I don't know what that is, but please do it.

"'In addition, Josephine, there are three accounts—one personal checking and two savings. The total of those accounts is one hundred and twenty-three thousand dollars and will be transferred over to your name.

"As for the store, it has been arranged for Jim to be bought out in the event of his death, which has happened. This was decided because none of you know anything about running a business. Josephine, you can expect an additional check for one hundred twenty thousand dollars from the sale forty-five days after the paperwork is complete, which will be on next Tuesday.

"Josephine, the title of the Cadillac will be transferred to your name upon final payment.

Diane, June, Honey and Jim Jr., each one of you will receive ten thousand dollars when you turn twenty-five. He said he chose this age because you'll have a better head on your shoulders than eighteen."

"Jane," he said, clearing his throat, "Jane, there is a separate life insurance policy of which Michael is the sole beneficiary for fifty thousand dollars. The car you currently drive, which is paid for, will be transferred to your name, and you will receive ten thousand dollars to help you transition from losing financial support from Jim. Lastly, the property at 107 Hummingbird Lane is in Jim's name, and according to Ohio state law, the house technically belongs to Josephine, but he willed it to her legally anyway. The law will provide you thirty days to relinquish the property or purchase it from Josephine if she is willing to sell it to you.
And that concludes the reading."

"Wait, that's it? Jim left me ten thousand dollars and a car? What am I supposed to do? That's my house—our house. What do you mean I have thirty days to relinquish? This makes absolutely no sense. Jim wouldn't have done this. He would have made sure I was taken care of."

"Oh, it makes perfect sense. You're a whore. You're the other woman! You don't have any rights. You weren't married to him. You were somebody he apparently was screwing." Diane stood, leaning over the table into Jane's face. "I hope you realize exactly what you were to him." She paused and looked down at her. "Well, I'll put it nicely: nobody. You meant nothing to him. You were a piece of tail."

"That's enough, Diane." Josephine put her hand on Diane's arm.

"You're right, Momma. It is enough. Enough of Daddy's BS. Who does she think she is? Trifling whore!"

"Now, I said it's enough."

Michael looked scared. "Why are you being so mean? I remember you. You used to be nice."

He was so precious and so sweet and innocent, trapped in a grownup's world.

Josephine stood. "I'm not going to deal with this now. Carl, I'll be in touch to figure out what's best. It's just too much to take in in one day." She thought to herself, it was bad enough Jim had Jane, but to find out he had another child, one that she wondered if he wanted, if it was planned, unlike the unwanted pregnancies she'd endured to bring her children here. She couldn't help but wonder what Jane's life was like with Jim. It seemed quite different than hers.

Diane looked at Michael. "I'm sorry if I scared you. None of this is your fault. You're too little to understand any of this, but one day you will." She looked over at Jane. "And I am sorry he has to live that truth. Although who knows, I'm sure you'll think of some outlandish story to make it all seem nice, White and right, won't you now? Bye, Michael. You'll be okay, remember that."

June got up and walked toward the door. "You have no idea the type of man my father really was. You couldn't, or you wouldn't be so shocked. You, my friend, are as my sister put it, a piece of tail." She let out a small laugh of satisfaction. "And if it wasn't for your son, you probably wouldn't be getting a thing." She smirked and shook her head. "So stupid," she mumbled under her breath and laughed.

Honey didn't see anything funny. She was confused and, in a way, felt sorry for Jane. She sat there thinking, *She is so dumb.* She was dumb if she thought Jim cared about anyone but himself.

"Sorry, Miss Jane," Jim Jr blurted out as he walked out. "Maybe I'll see you around one day, Michael."

No one read their letters there except Jane. Diane and June scoffed at theirs and stuffed them down in their purses.

"I'll leave you to yourself. Take as long as you need," Carl said and stepped out.

That's exactly what she did. She took almost an hour sitting there as if the longer she sat, the will would be different. "I'm ready to go, Mommy," Michael said repeatedly in his exhausted seven-year-old voice before Jane composed herself enough to step foot outside the office into her new reality. She held the letter tightly in one hand with Michael's hand in the other. Making her way to the car, she tried to fight back the tears. What was she going to do?

They got to the car, and after getting in, she was frozen in time again until Michael jarred her back to reality once again.

"Give me a minute, honey. Mommy is having a rough day."

"Is it because Daddy is gone away to heaven?"

"Yes, baby." She sighed. "It's because Daddy is gone away to heaven, and Mommy doesn't know what she's going to do without him."

"You have me, Mommy." He looked up at her with those big, round eyes. "I'll never leave you."

"Yes, I sure do, and you're the best thing that could have ever happened to Mommy." Her eyes filled with tears.

"Then why are you crying?"

"Sometimes grownups just cry to feel better."

"Well, you should be feeling pretty great, Mommy, because you've been crying a lot."

She couldn't help but laugh. "Okay. Give Mommy one more minute, and then we're going to go to Grandma's and have some lunch."

She took a deep breath as she unsealed the letter.

Jane,

What can I say other than I am sorry I have apparently left you?

I need you to know some things that you might be puzzled about.

I love you, Jane, and as long as we were together, I would do whatever I could for you, but ain't no way I was gonna leave you a lot of money to be enjoying with another man. I update my will every year, and at the time of this here letter, you still young enough to meet somebody

else and live your life, which I expect you to do. Only thing is he gon' have to bring his own money to the table. You ain't gonna be livin' high on the hog from the sweat of my brow. I ain't havin' none of that.

Quite frankly, I can't trust you, Jane. You changed on me. We was in this thing together and then you went and tried to start changing things on me, like what we had wasn't good enough. I know you got pregnant with Michael on purpose, even after we talked about it time and time again and I told you no. I ain't no dummy. Now you know I have a lot of connections, Jane. I sent somebody to the pharmacy and paid him and the pharmacist some good money to do a little diggin'. I had to send somebody because you know they wasn't gon' tell me nothin' and would probably call the cops on me. But the right White man in his expensive suit and wad of money can find out

anything he wanna know. Guess what he found out, Jane? You hadn't
got your birth control filled in five months.

Now go figure. So see, Janie, I can't trust you. Now
Josephine, see, her I can trust. All the hell I put her through, she ain't
never once talked bad about me, left me. Hell, she was probably too
good for me. She deserves everything I got cause I didn't do her right,
and I know I didn't, and as much as I loved you, Jane, something in
me changed when I found out you tricked me. Now Michael is my son,
so I want him to be alright. He innocent. He ain't try to trick me. He
just caught in the middle, so when he get old enough and got a little
sense in his head, I want him to have some money to start his life.
Well, for whatever reason God saw fit to take me out the earth, but
you gon' be okay. Get you a nice White man who don't mind that
you've been touched by me and made a baby and get that normal
relationship you been after.

Love you even in the afterlife,
Jim

This is how Jane and Jim's relationship ended. They were not
married but death did them apart.

Are We Being Punished?

Diane's Story

D uring the visit home, Diane sat on the end of Josephine's bed, and she turned to her.

"I really need to tell you something about Jim."

When she continued to speak, Josephine motioned her to stop. "No need in rehashing old things."

"But, Momma, I really need to tell you something."

"Í said hush now, Diane. I mean." Josephine was firm.

"But you don't understand."

"I understand plenty. You don't think I know you probably have stuff you want to get off your chest about Jim? Everyone in this house probably does, but Diane, I just do not want to live in the past, and I hope you can understand that. If it's about your father, I know it can't be good, and I just can't take anymore. I had to battle to get free and I can't go back."

Diane had paid a hard price for being exposed too young to things a girl shouldn't be and taking on being an adult long before time. She had to protect her family. She knew she wasn't the oldest, but she was the toughest. She could stand up for herself, and she was not afraid of anyone. She had gone to Georgia with one thing on her mind, a new life—a chance to start fresh and to right the wrongs of those who had no voice.

Becoming a lawyer was her way to advocate for women. Though she tried to escape the demons of what had gone on in that home growing up, they followed her. She couldn't stand to see a woman beaten or raped, and she fought hard to give these women a voice. It was only recently most states even considered non-consensual sex with a wife rape. A woman had no defense.

Diane remembered the first time she heard Jim rape Josephine. It was late, and she was startled from her sleep by her mother's cries. Diane could tell her mother was trying not to wake anyone, but she knew something wasn't right. She could hear Jim slap her.

"Open your legs, I said."

Josephine pleaded with him that he was hurting her and to just calm down and give her a minute because she was in pain from the beating he had just whaled on her. Diane tried to open the door, but it was locked. She banged on the door, yelling, "Open the door. Momma. Are you okay? Open this door."

June came running down the hall questioning what was going on.

"He's going to kill her, June. I can tell. We have to do something."

"Diane, just go back to bed. Momma can take care of herself." "Yeah, right. What do you mean? Does she sound like she can take care of herself?" "You can go. I'm okay."

I'm not leaving until he opens this door," she screamed as she hit the door. "Open the door, Momma."

"Get away from the door before I come out there," Jim screamed.

"Come on! Just let my mother outta there," June pleaded.

He swung the door open with a fierce rage in his eyes. He was sweating and smelled like alcohol. He grabbed Diane by the arm. "You wanna take her place?"

She was stunned, not by his words, but by the image of her half-naked beaten mother. She tried to run into the room, but he picked her up and tossed her to the wall.

"I'm fine, Diane. Go back to bed."

He slammed the door.

When she began to practice law, she made it her mission to help every woman she could, and in 1985, it was no longer legal for a husband to rape his wife. Domestic violence was still a bit trickier. She had seen it all: helping women fight to get away from their abusive husbands only to see them return to the abuser. A man actually getting convicted of spousal abuse was a rare victory, and even if only a minimal sentence, it was progress—progress that was needed. She didn't want to be a man, be equal to a man nor did she want to do anything a man could do, but what she wanted was rights. She believed a woman should have the same rights as a man to not be beaten, taken advantage of, preyed upon, objectified or degraded because she wasn't a man. She had the right to go to school and pursue her dreams and have the same opportunity available when she graduated.

Luckily, she had a man beside her who supported these dreams. She didn't know if she was a feminist or not, but she knew women needed advocates who weren't afraid to pave the way, so she rallied when she could and marched when necessary and fought for the voiceless and didn't care what it cost her. Richard rallied with her. Though sometimes he felt she'd gone too far, he loved her and wanted her to be happy. He often didn't understand her passion and didn't understand when she would sometimes withdraw, but he gave her space and loved her unconditionally.

Sometimes when you don't really know what love looks like through the damaged lens of your life, you don't really know how to receive the blessing of this love. The love that heals instead of hurts, that compromises instead of demands, that gives instead of takes, and Richard was all these things, even when she was ever suspicious. He was her man as much as she would allow him to be.

He never knew much about her childhood—little bits and pieces she had divulged to him, but never enough for him to know the type of trauma she had experienced. He knew her father was a little rough sometimes with her mother and that he had attempted to provide a good financial life for them and that he was killed when she was younger.

He wanted the two of them to be all in. He wanted to know more, but she rarely talked about specifics unless it had something to do with June and Honey. Sometimes they would be laying on the couch watching television or sitting at the table eating, and it was as if something would pull a trigger inside her, and she would just excuse herself with no explanation.

As she and Richard were sitting on the porch, talking and laughing, he jokingly said, "If I tell you to, you will. Now go in there and fix my dinner, woman." He went to pull her in to him and hug her, and she snatched away and went in the house.

"Are you serious? You know I was joking, babe." He continued to laugh, thinking he would explain and everything would be okay.

Diane quickly went upstairs and locked herself in the bathroom and tried to tune everything out. She tried to make sense of what was transpiring as she would each time. What he said had taken her back to Jim, and when Jim said those kinds of things he meant them. There was no joking. She refused to allow herself to be dominated by anyone. She loved Richard, but she could never fully let him in—after all, in her mind, he was a man. Even if he was a good man today, it didn't mean he would stay that way. Jim had started out good, hadn't he? Josephine had shared broken images of the man she had come to know and love. She made attempts to piece together the good—she had a way of doing that with everyone. Diane hadn't picked up that gift.

She hated Jim. Even all those years later, she hated him.

There was a soft knock on the door, "Hey, *ummm,* I'm not sure what just happened. Are we good? Did I do something? You know I was just messing with you, right?"

"I'm okay. I just need a minute."

"A minute to what? Diane, I love you. You've gotta let me in. You know we're on the same team, fighting for the same causes. I would never do anything to hurt you. I just never know what's going to set you off, and I can't not be me."

"I can't not be me either, Richard. I said just give me a minute." *Why did I just snap at him like that?* she thought. She sat there beating herself up. She heard the garage door open, and shortly after, his car started up, and he was gone. She came out of the bathroom and called June, who didn't answer. She had a few girlfriends in Atlanta, but no one who could relate or identify or who knew her story. She didn't think she was embarrassed—it was more so shame. Jim had violated her, and she never told a soul. It was payback for her standing up to him for Josephine.

She remembered it like it was yesterday. She had come home from school. Josephine was in the kitchen washing greens, and Jim was sitting in the front room watching television.

"Well, if it isn't mouth almighty waltzing in my house like she got rights," Jim said.

She ignored him, went straight up to her room and took her books out to start her homework. Soon after, she heard Jim's footsteps coming down the hall. She didn't know why, but her heart started to beat fast. He opened her room door and just stood in the doorway.

"I got something to fix you." He smirked. "Think you gon' live under my roof and disrespect me," he mumbled.

Diane didn't move. She sat there and continued acting as if she was doing her homework.

"Aye, you hear me talking to you? Look at me when I talk to you!" She refused to look at him. "You think you somebody, don't you? You gon' learn just like your momma learned. You what I tell you you can be." She still refused to look up. He walked over and knocked her books off the desk onto the floor. She sat still refusing to look at him. He grabbed her face and turned it toward his. "You just wait. You lucky your momma home." He pushed her face. "Clean this mess up." He turned and walked away.

What did he mean by that? Was he going to beat her if Josephine wasn't there? For the next few months, he verbally tortured her when no one was paying attention, but she wouldn't cower down. Sitting there on the side of the bed, wishing June would pick up, she wondered why she just didn't swallow her pride, but she couldn't. He was wrong and awful, and someone had to stand up to him, right?

She questioned herself as if she could go back and change it. Even if she could, she probably wouldn't have. She dealt with the torment, refusing to tell Josephine because she didn't want to put any more on her mind.

One night Diane was headed out with her friends. Josephine and Honey were gone with Mabel, June was gone to the movies, and Jim Jr. was staying over at a friend's.

"Where you think you're going?" Jim questioned.

"Out with Sabrina and Rachel" She resented him even asking her anything. She could tell he was drunk. All she wanted to do was get out the house. She headed for the door to wait outside for Sabrina to get there. "Aye, get me another drink before you leave."

"I can't. Sabrina is gonna be here any minute. I told her I would be outside."

"Do what you're told. Sabrina can wait."

She let out a sigh and walked over to the bar in the dining room to make his drink. "Can't stand him," she mumbled under her breath.

"You better watch that attitude, I done told you," he growled at her.

"Here." She set the drink on the table.

"Give it to me."

"You can't get that glass right there?"

"I'm tired of your mouth."

As she turned to walk away, he purposely knocked the glass over. She was so pissed at herself because she knew she would have to clean it up, and all she wanted to do was get out of there.

"Look at you. Make me another one, and clean that mess up."

Her anger kindled as she slammed the ice in the glass. "Here." She handed it to him. She went and got a towel to sop up the mess. She put the ice cubes from the table in the glass as Jim laughed. She heard a zipper, and the next thing she knew he was behind her pulling her dress up.

"What are you doing? You're drunk stop. Get off me!" she yelled.

"Shut up! You're gonna learn to respect me. I'm tired of you."

He held her down to the floor until he was done. She refused to cry. She wouldn't give him the satisfaction. She just laid there.

"Get up and go clean up before somebody come home. I ain't worried about you tellin' yo' momma. She can't do nothin'. Remember, this all started because you was trying to save her, so how she gonna save you?" He stepped over her and went upstairs. "I hope that will teach you some manners and remind you who the boss is."

She knew he was right. What good would tellin' her mother do? She buried it deep, deep down inside and never spoke of it. It never happened again, but once was enough. After that day, every time she got out of line, he would just simply say, "Do you need a lesson?"

If only she had known, June was taught that very same lesson that day he made her come in off the swing. It wasn't that June was as meek as Diane had painted her in her mind, but he held that same threat over her head, and she never wanted to experience anything like that again, so she conformed and got out as soon as she could.

Diane didn't want to mess up her relationship with Richard, but it seemed as if she was destined to do just that. She didn't know how to be vulnerable, and though she wanted to learn with Richard, it was hard. The third year of marriage, they got pregnant, and it was exciting—until she entered the second trimester. Sitting at her desk at work, she felt some mild cramping, almost like menstrual cramps, but she didn't think much of it. The cramps slightly worsened, so she stood to go to the restroom. When she stood and felt a small warm gush, she knew what was happening. She grabbed several paper towels and got a pad out of the wall machine before entering the stall. Thankfully, no one else was in there.

Leaning against the stall wall, she sucked up the tears. "Don't cry. Do not cry, Diane. Everything is fine. Things happen." She sighed. "Suck it up. It's fine." She hovered over the toilet for a while before cleaning up and pulling herself together. She stared at herself in the mirror, questioning why before reminding herself how strong she was. "You don't have time for a baby anyway. You're savin' the world." She smiled at herself before going back to her office and calling her doctor.

"Dr. Cavanough's office. This is Mandi. How can I help you?"

"Hello, this is Diane Holloway. I need to see if Dr. Cavanough can see me today."

"Unfortunately, she cannot. What are you needing to be seen for?"

"Well, I believe I just had a miscarriage about twenty minutes ago, and I just wanted to come in and have her take a look," she said very matter of fact with a slight bit of sarcasm.

"Oh my goodness, I am so sorry. Just come in. We will work you in."

She hung up the phone and let her secretary know she was leaving for the day. Driving down the highway, she thought she should have called Richard before she left the office, but she truly had not thought about it.

The doctor confirmed she'd had a miscarriage. She was fine though. The doctor talked to her about possibly seeing a therapist because losing a child could be devastating, but she declined as she felt perfectly fine.

"It's just not the right time, I guess. It's really okay, Dr. Cavanough. I'm okay." She smiled.

"Diane, there is nothing wrong with acknowledging the pain of the loss. You don't have to be strong. We are here to support you."

"I said I'm fine."

Later at home, sitting at the table drinking a cup of coffee, she pondered how Richard would take the news. He was so excited about the baby. It had been good for a relationship that was already great. She was still sitting there two hours later when he arrived home.

"Hey, baby." His face always lit up when he saw her.

"Hey, baby."

He could tell something wasn't right. He walked over to the table, setting his briefcase down. "What's up, babe? You okay?"

"I lost the baby," she said, expressionless.

"Wait. What? Why didn't you call me at the office? Diane, we know you're strong. Everyone knows you're strong, but we need each other. This affects me, too, not just because it was my baby, but because you're my wife, and whatever you go through, I go through. What can I do?"

"Nothing. There's nothing we can do, Richard." She looked hopeless, a look she rarely had. She was Diane the strong.

He stood, took her by the hand and led her up to the sun porch. He sat down and motioned for her to sit with him with her head in his lap. She wanted to cry, she wanted to break down, but something in her wouldn't allow for it.

"I love you," she said softly.

"Love you too." He continued to rub her head. "Everything is going to be okay."

There was another miscarriage the following year and one final one that same year, this one close to the end of the fifth month, and it was hard on them both. Diane was on bedrest the better part of this pregnancy as a precaution, but it didn't matter. Laying on the couch watching television, she felt some minor cramping.

"God no! Please, please don't let it happen again. Please."

Her nerves began to get the better of her. She tried to relax and breathe, and it seemed to help a bit, and eventually the cramps subsided.

"Okay. Maybe I'm worried for no reason. Everything is going to be fine." The self-talk continued to soothe her, but she was afraid to move but after a while she had to pee. When she stood, the cramping continued and worsened as she walked toward the bathroom. She stopped and called Richard at his office.

"Baby, I think it's happening again." She began to weep.

He sat back in his chair, putting his fist to his forehead, attempting to sound reassuring and comforting. "It's going to be fine. Calm down. I'm leaving now, okay?"

"Okay." She made her way to the bathroom and peed. There was no blood. This was reassuring. She laid back down on the couch and waited for Richard.

Twenty minutes later he came flying through the door. "How are you? What's going on?" He kneeled on the floor next to the couch.

"I think I'm okay. The cramping stopped. I'm sorry I got you worried. I just got so scared."

"Don't be sorry. I'm here. We're in this together." He leaned in real close to her belly and spoke softly. "Alright in there. We're excited to see you, too, but it's not quite time yet. You need to stay in a bake a little longer so you will be perfect. Okay? Do we have a deal?"

Diane looked down at him. He was so wonderful and gentle, and he was everything she could have ever hoped for in a man. She thought surely this little one would listen to his/her daddy, but later that same night, she awoke to cramping pains tearing through her stomach.

"*Ahhh,* Richard! Richard! Get up! I need to go to the hospital now." She cried out.

Stunned out of his sleep, he jumped up, threw on some sweats and a T-shirt. He grabbed her robe and threw is around her and picked her up. There was blood in the bed, but he didn't alarm her. He tried to assure her it would be okay. The cramping continued as they made their way to the hospital. He pulled into the ER and ran and asked for a wheelchair. There wasn't much that could be done. Diane was losing a lot of blood, but they gave her something in an attempt to stop her uterus from contracting.

The nurse attempted to find a heartbeat but was having a hard time. Eventually there was a faint beat and a sigh of relief as the doctor came in to ask questions and provide options. The hope was to keep the baby in as long as possible, but no matter what they tried, she kept going into labor. The chances of the baby surviving at five months were so slim, and technology wasn't what it is today.

The labor was horrible, and Steven, which is what they named him, lived seven hours, and he was beautiful, but just wasn't strong enough to take on the world. That little angel decided he would rather stay up in heaven, and Diane and Richard made peace with that. Diane, however, could not bring herself to try anymore. She would take her punishment as it was dished out. Deep in her heart, she knew God wasn't really punishing her, but it sure felt like it.

Weeks later, she sat on the sunporch dazed and confused wondering about this thing called life and exactly how people were supposed to live it. She wanted to go to church, but she couldn't. Diane had not stepped foot in a church since she had moved out of her mother's home. She didn't want to be a hypocrite, and she couldn't quite wrap her head around God's forgiveness of all sin, especially not hers, but if he was up there keeping tabs aren't they even? Shouldn't they have been even after the first loss?

She wanted to cry out, but her screams were frozen inside, so the silence grew louder, and as much as Richard tried to be there, she couldn't allow him to be. She loved him so much, and she knew one of the things he always talked about was having a family and being a dad. He was so looking forward to it, and she couldn't take that from him. She did everything she could to sabotage the marriage until she finally told him it would never work and that he needed to be with someone who could give him what she couldn't.

Richard tried to stay. He was fine adopting, but Diane couldn't take the chance of him one day resenting her, so after eight years of the perfect love story, it was over. Her heart was broken, but that's all she had known her entire life, so she was used to it. She was one of the sweetest, most beautiful people you could know. She would do anything to help someone but inside she was broken, hurting and angry, but no one would ever know. This was her secret, among many others.

She worked tirelessly to try and change laws and make the system work for those who were often getting the short end of the stick, and this became her life. She opened three battered women's shelters, and her good surely outweighed her bad, and no matter how much good she did, her bad always seemed to visit her in her thoughts and nightmares. Her inner self would betray her and tell her she could never do enough good to make it go away, and this made her work even harder at being better, doing more, sacrificing all. The good works had to outweigh the sin, but if she believed everything she had been taught in church, her good deeds had nothing to do with God forgiving her. She knew she just had to repent, but true repentance meant being sorry, and she simply wasn't sorry. Her sin was quite intentional, and she would do it again in a heartbeat.

Did this make her a bad person? This was the question she wrestled with most of her adult life. Knowing life wasn't fair didn't give anyone the right to change someone's fate, but that's exactly what she did every day, so why was it permissible in that instance and not in others? Some days she was numb while others she carried the fiery torch of the many who needed her help, but there was never enough help to erase the pains of her past.

Are We Being Punished?

June's Story

B ack at the house, June's phone wouldn't stop ringing. Honey and Diane both wondered why she wouldn't answer it, but neither wanted to ask. Acting as if her phone wasn't vibrating continuously, she asked Diane how long she planned on staying, but Diane wasn't sure. She knew eventually she had to get back to work, but she wanted to make sure Josephine was okay. The phone rang again.

Irritated, Diane blurted out, "For God's sake, answer the phone, June."

She simply replied no and continued with their conversation.

"Why won't you answer?" Honey inquired.

"You guys are so nosey. It's Charlie," she said, referring to the musician she had run off with years ago.

Honey and Diane looked at one another and then back at June.

"Wow, that's a blast from the past. What's that about?" Diane asked.

"He wants to see me. Apparently, he's been clean for three years, and he claims he's never loved anyone but me."

"Hmmm." Honey smiled. "Well, are you going to see him?

"No! No, I'm not going to see him. He's part of my past—a past I want to leave far, far behind." Her eyes glazed over as she remembered bits and pieces of the shell of a life she shared with a man she thought she loved. But how was she to know what love was? She had never seen a true form of it, and she couldn't count on the movies and television to enlighten her. What she knew was unhealthy, and though she tried to find love, it always eluded her. Now she was in a healthy place, had a new zeal for life and something she had never had before: a relationship with God. The girls had gone to church their whole lives, but none of them could wrap their heads around a God who would allow the hell they had experienced in their lives to be real and love them like the preacher said he did.

Sunday after Sunday, they dressed in their Sunday's best, loaded into the car and drove to the Pentecostal church they had been raised in. They each had a different take on God and who he was—if he was. June had seen the most the longest, and though she enjoyed the choir singing, and it sometimes brought her to tears, the tears weren't because she was being moved by the spirit, but instead because she knew when the perfected front the family portrayed in the public eye would shatter once they reached home and the front door to their house closed. The most frustrating part was she never knew when it would happen or even why, but whatever demons Jim fought with inside of himself always seemed to win. So even though for the longest time, she didn't believe in God, she surely believed in the devil. She had come to know him well. She just always prayed his seed didn't take root in her. She never wanted to be anything like her father, and truth be told, as much as she loved her mother, she didn't want to be like her either. The sad thing was running from her father's sins landed her in her own sins.

No one could ever know what she had experienced in Los Angeles. Everyone saw the palm trees, sun and celebrities, and they thought, *Hey, I would love to be there to live that life,* but they didn't know the other side—the side that didn't make it onto the covers of magazines and entertainment news, the people who came with hopes and dreams, and out of all the hopefuls, not many made it. But what was making it? Even some of those who made it lost themselves to the beast that is Hollywood. June could only imagine what she may have done for a line if her habit wasn't supported, but she did do things that were out of character for her: sleeping with women— something she had never entertained the thought of—and multiple partners, not even able to remember half the things she allowed people to do with her body while she was getting high.

The one thing she did remember was being sick, so sick she couldn't even stand some days. Finally, Melissa, her best friend, made her go to the doctor. She didn't want to go because she didn't want to be judged—judged for her lifestyle, her choices and her addiction. She had no choice. She wasn't getting any better, and even when she was high, it didn't take her mind off the spurts off sickness. She was pregnant, and she didn't know who the father was at this point. She felt embarrassed, dirty and ashamed. She cried out to Melissa. As much as she believed she loved Charlie, having sex with other men had sometimes occurred.

"How can I not even know who the father is? I'm so trifling."

"It's going to be okay. Don't cry. You aren't the first woman in the world who isn't certain who the father of their child is, and you certainly won't be the last. I mean I'm just saying, women who are Goody Two-shoes slip up every now and then and have to try to count the weeks and days and hope they come up with the right answer."

She rocked her friend as she sobbed. Besides, it was LA in the eighties. During that time, there was a lot of parties, a lot of drugs and a lot of sex. She wasn't alone in this. It was just that she'd gotten pregnant.

At the follow-up appointment, the doctor estimated the baby to be seventeen weeks. She continued to beat herself up for not having any idea she was pregnant, and even worse, not being able to stop using. She remembered sitting at the table trying to read a magazine and think about not getting high. It was that much worse now because she knew she couldn't. It was an intense battle she would eventually lose most days. Charlie came in, plopped down at the table and began prepping his lines. Watching him snort coke made her want some so bad. She had been clean this time for a whole four days. She was determined to do right by the baby, but it was killing her.

"Do you have to do that right here?" she asked, but he just ignored her and continued.

"Here. Come on. A little bit won't hurt, and it'll relax you because quite frankly you've been a bitch ever since you found out about this bastard baby that probably ain't even mine."

The words cut deeper than any knife ever could because he was right, but this was his fault. He had introduced her to this world of pain that started out so fun. From the first time when she met him, she felt alive and untouchable. There was no Jim around. She had escaped one prison only to turn her striped jumpsuit in for an orange one. As hard as she tried, she continued to use, not as heavily as she had, but it was enough for premature labor. She was high and tested positive for cocaine when they admitted her, and at only thirty-two weeks, she delivered a three-pound, four-ounce baby girl who was immediately taken to the intensive care unit.

The very next day, a social worker came in to see her. She was irritable and sad. For the safety of the baby, she wasn't allowed to breastfeed nor was she allowed to be alone with the baby. Melissa sat there with her. She was advised Child Protective Services would be placing the baby in temporary care of the state. She heard all this, but she was in a fog. She needed to get high, but she wanted to see her baby.

"Ms. Holloway, do you understand what I'm saying to you?"

"Huh? Yes. You wanna take my baby away. That's it, right?"

"I don't want to take your baby, but under the circumstances, I have no choice. I have to do what's in the best interest of the child, and right now, I couldn't send this baby home with you, even when she does get out of the ICU. Her lungs are underdeveloped and cognitively speaking, we have to wait and see."

She wanted to see her, but she wanted to get high even more. "Yeah, maybe it's for the best, right?" She turned and looked at Melissa.

"Can I see her before I go home? I have to get out of here."

"Ms. Holloway, if you want to get your child, the best thing you can do for her is to get off the drugs. That's the only way you can take care of her properly. I can help you, but you have to be willing to commit to sobriety."

"I don't need a savior, okay? Just let me see her."

Melissa wheeled June down to the neonatal intensive care unit to see the smallest, most precious little life she would ever want to see, and they both wept. June couldn't touch her. She was so tiny and so fragile and hooked up to so many different machines.

"I am so sorry." She wept and placed her hand on the outside of the incubator. "So, so sorry." She looked at Melissa. "What have I done?"

Melissa held her and promised her it would be okay. "I'll help you. You're not alone."

"I want to go home. I can't be here anymore. I just need to go home."

The doctor discharged her though it wasn't recommended, but she didn't care. She signed herself out, and Melissa drove her home. When she arrived, Charlie was passed out on the floor where he had probably been from the prior night. She called his name, but there was no response.

She looked over at Melissa. "Do you have anything on you?"

"June, honestly, you'll never get your baby back if you don't straighten up."

"Who said I wanted her back?" she barked defensively. "I don't need a speech, I need to get high, okay?"

Melissa understood, but she left, slamming the door behind her. She didn't want to see June further destroy herself. Something about seeing June like that put things in perspective for her and was the first aha moment she had in taking steps toward her own sobriety. She offered to walk through it with June, but she wasn't ready, and you can't force someone to get clean. They have to want it for themselves, because it's a fight. A big ugly, dirty fight that you have to go a few rounds with until you finally win, if you win at all.

June went to the hospital every day to see Lalah—that's what she named her. The social worker tried to work with June. She offered to help her get into a program so she could get healthy enough to get Lalah when she was able to come home. She continually refused the help, which in the end didn't matter. Little precious Lalah lasted nine days before going into cardiac arrest and passing on to the next life. June wasn't there when it happened, but the hospital did call her, and she came.

She wept bitter tears as they placed Lalah's lifeless body in her hands. It was too much for her to bear. Her legs gave way from underneath her, and she tumbled to the floor as the nurse grabbed Lalah. This numbed June even more and caused her to want to be numb. She didn't want to face who she was becoming.

June had a small graveside service for Baby Lalah. She sat in a chair, Charlie on one side and Melissa on the other, thinking how she never even got a chance to hold her or smell her while she was alive, only after she was gone, and her eyes welled again with tears of fire. She remembered when Honey was a baby and Jim and Josephine had first brought her home. She smelled like new baby, soft and fresh and clean. It was an indescribable scent, mixed with feelings and emotion. Anyone who has ever smelled little bitty babies knows what an emotional smell is. Who had she become and how? She sat there for hours after everyone had gone. Charlie tried to comfort her, but there was no comfort to be found. She reached down in her purse and grabbed the small vial knowing that was the only thing that could dull the pain—the very thing that caused the pain was the pain remedy.

Eventually, she stood. She felt she was as numb as she could possibly get, and she began to laugh.

"Well, you really did it now, June. Can't get much worse than this. Even God knows I'm not meant to be a mother. I think I could have been a good mother. Just not today. But one day, God, will you let me be a mommy?" she pleaded like a little girl asking for something from her parents. Tears flowed down her face hitting her dress. She turned to Charlie, and he just held her as she wept an eternal weep that could never be soothed.

"This is your fault. I wish I never would have met you!" She began hitting and slapping him wildly.

He just took it and tried to grab her and hold her. "It's probably for the best. Look at you! June look at us. Do you think we could be somebody's parents?"

She sank to the ground and lay there motionless. "I guess not," she said softly. "I guess not."

He picked her up and walked her to the car, and they went back to live life as they once knew it before the great tragedy—back to the parties, shopping, wine and dining and more coke to numb life itself. June was never really the same, but she continued.

No one in her family knew. That was a different life, a life she didn't want to remember, and Charlie was a clear reminder of the pain she buried way down deep inside.

"You don't even just want to see what he has to say?" Honey asked.

June shut her eyes real tight and growled, "No." She balled her fists and pounded them on the bed. "Have you ever been tired, Honey? Have you?" She stared her in the eyes. "I mean real tired." Her lips began to tremble. "I was tired and alone, and most days I couldn't breathe, and you could never understand what that's like—when you're afraid but don't even know why. When you don't want to close your eyes because you know you're going to wake up, and you close them anyway and pray to God they never open again. But if by chance they do, open that is, when they open, you hope to be in an entirely different place, another realm, and you pray to have no memories of your pain, frustration and failures. So no, Honey, no I'm not going to see what he wants. I can't care what he wants because there's a slight chance if I care I'll end up in that very dark place I crawled and fought my way out of, and he's a reminder of that place. So again—" she rose from the bed filled with furry—"some things are better left in the past. I would think you would have learned that. I was dead inside, and no one could save me." She left the room.

"Wow...*ummm,* okay, then." Honey looked over at Diane, confused. "What was that? Is there something I'm missing? Do you know something I don't?"

"No. I mean you knew she partied a lot when she was with him and that she wasn't herself, but I have no idea exactly what this dark place she crawled out of is. I mean, I know she was dabbling with drugs and drinking a lot, but I don't think it was super serious. Maybe it was, I don't know. You know she doesn't like to talk about that part of her life, so I don't press it, but I know she loved Charlie, or at least I think she did. I still don't know the whole story behind that, but I think we need to just leave it alone, at least for right now anyway. Besides, we need to focus on Momma."

They sat a few more minutes talking about what the next steps would be and how they would convince Josephine she was in fact not that old, and just because her best friend had died, she didn't have to die with her.

A True Friend

J osephine and Mabel had done it all. She had been there with
Josephine through the rough times with Jim, and after she would
say her peace about a thing, she left it there, and that's what made
their friendship so strong, She never could understand Josephine
staying with that fool Jim, but she never judged, never pushed, and
anytime she was needed, she was there with no questions asked.
That's what friends did: Even if they didn't agree with your decisions,
they agreed they were just that, your decisions, and your friends were
just that and that meant no matter what.

Josephine liked that Mabel was always honest with her, but
that she knew when to just let stuff go. Besides, all the words in the
world weren't going to change either of their minds about Jim.
Josephine was for him, and Mabel was definitely against him. Jim
knew it, too, and sometimes he tried to keep them apart, but after a
while, he figured she had to have something, and one thing Mabel
never was was disrespectful to Jim in his house. No matter how much
she disliked him, she was raised not to disrespect a man in his own
home. If you didn't like the way they lived or the things they did, you
stayed away, simple as that.

Some days, the anger would boil up inside of her the way he
often spoke to Josephine, and sometimes she saw the consequences of
his anger across her face or on her arms. She could never understand
it. She had seen it once or twice in her own family growing up, and
she refused to ever let a man put his hands on her, and she didn't. If a

man even looked at her like he could possibly one day in the distant future think he might want to put his hands on her, that relationship was over real quick. It was a wonder she ever got married, but she did, and Mike McCary had never once put his hands up to her.

Mike and Mabel were what a relationship should be, and Diane often looked at them and wanted that so badly for her own mother and just couldn't understand why her mother didn't want it for herself. It was so hard on Josephine when Mabel died, She was only fifty-eight. It was a long five months. That's all it took for cancer to ravage her body.

Josephine was there every step of the way—through chemo, through hope, though shattered hope when Mabel left. Josephine lay in the bed with Mabel many days, but the last day was the best and the worse. They laughed as they reminisced about the lives they had lived and the friendship they had built over the nearly forty years they had come to know each other.

"Remember when I taught you how to drive that summer behind Ole Jim Boy's back?"

They both laughed.

"He sure was mad at you, Mabel. The funny thing is I knew how to drive a little but when I met Jim, he always took me everywhere, and I was too blind to see he was setting me up to depend solely on him. Girl, shoot, him leaving this earth was bittersweet. I loved him until he beat it out of me. I mean Jim could be good when he wanted. He just... I don't know, Mabel"

She stared off into nothing envisioning the Jim she knew when they first met. "He just had too many demons, and he fed them instead of getting free from them, you know?" She looked over at Mabel.

"Yeah, Josephine, I know. Life is funny like that sometimes. You can have in your head who you wanna be, but sometimes it's too hard to be that, so you just follow that ole devil right to hell. He had Ole Jim Boy tricked. He coulda had it all—good wife, good kids, just a good life—but...well, never mind. It's all water under the bridge. Maybe I'll see 'im when I get up there. Maybe God had some mercy on his sick soul, you know? It ain't for us to say who gettin' in and who ain't." Mabel stared up at the ceiling.

"*Hmmm.* Yeah." Josephine teared up. "What am I going to do without you, Mabel? I mean, really? I keep praying for a miracle. Some days I think I need the miracle more for me than for you because you're all I've got."

She laid her head on Mabel's pillow as the tears burned her eyes.

"Alright, alright. That's enough of this. Get me up. I wanna go sit outside. I need to feel the sun on my face. I wonder if it's going to be sunny in glory all the time and exactly what we're gonna be doin' up there for all eternity."

They both laughed as Josephine wiped her eyes and got Mabel's wheelchair ready.

"*Hmmm.* I know what they better have: your apple pie, Mabel. When I get up there, it ain't gonna be heaven without some of your

apple pie. Even with the recipe, I can't make it like you, I just can't."
She laughed.

Mabel's husband gave them their time and space. He knew
Mabel was really all Josephine had after the girls moved away. He
would listen outside the door sometimes as they talked and cried, and
it helped him not be so sad to have Josephine share the burden of
losing her with him. At night, he would cry silently at the kitchen
table, always putting on his best face for Mabel, who knew he was
hurting. She never expected to die this soon. They were supposed to
grow old together sitting on their porch waiting for their
grandchildren they didn't have yet to come visit.

They were blessed to have one daughter when Mabel was
thirty-six after trying for years, and she was the sunshine of their
lives. She was away at college, and they refused to tell her how bad
things were. She was in her senior year at Spelman, and they didn't
want her to leave school when she was so close to finishing, but when
it got really bad, they knew they had to tell her or she would never
forgive them.

When Candace arrived home and saw how frail and weak her
mother was, it almost killed her. It simply wasn't fair. She ended up
not returning for her last semester until the following fall. There was
no way she could be so far away knowing her mother was literally
dying. She refused to die in the hospital and stayed home right until
the very end. Surrounded by Mike, Candace, Josephine and Mabel's
mother, it was just a matter of time, and they all knew it. The

morphine kept her comfortable the last few weeks, but this day, her breathing was labored, and they knew it wouldn't be long.

They were solemn but glad she would no longer be in pain, and Josephine who wasn't a drinker took a drink when Mike offered it. She kissed her friend softly on the forehead and whispered in her ear, "I'll see you on the other side, friend." This was the greatest loss she had ever experienced, and she never wanted to know this pain again.

Honey's Story

That night, Honey was talking to her fiancé Jared on the phone trying to have him help her make sense of all that was transpiring. He explained June's odd behavior and how there was actually nothing wrong with her mother but that she wanted to just die, which of course she couldn't wrap her head around. He was totally on board with her moving to New York with them, but they both knew she would never agree to that, just based on her personality. She went on to explain how nothing is as it seems. They were all still close, but Honey described it as something weird going on that she couldn't verbalize but that she could feel. Jared decided he needed to come there, but Honey said it wasn't necessary, so he didn't.

She lay on her childhood bed thinking about her childhood and wondering what the purpose was. Why was their house the house of torture? Why couldn't it be normal like other kids, and why after Jim was killed and she was free didn't her mother find someone to love her the way she knew how to love? She sometimes felt guilty because her life had turned out so good. Not that she hadn't had a hiccup here and there, like the time Jared almost left her.

Some days she wondered if she really loved Jared or instead what he was to her. He was a provider, and he loved her, and they had fun together, but he was old on the inside. He was all the things a man should be when it came to respect and responsibility, and they were definitely financially stable, but Honey loved flying by the seat of her pants, and Jared was a planner. He was logical but never had a problem with Honey hanging out and traveling and whatever else she wanted to do, and truth be told, the real reason behind Flight, her dance studio, was Honey proving she could actually settle herself after her relationship with Kent. It wasn't a sexual relationship. It was far worse. He was in her head, and before long, he was in her heart and began to make her second guess her relationship with Jared. It wasn't intentional on his part. It was just one of those things.

She met him at a coffee shop after a performance in Europe, he lived in Chicago. They were both hired as part of a company that was performing overseas for three months. Honey was doing what she loved six days a week, and the seventh day, she and Kent would sightsee and laugh and talk and eat and drink coffee in little cafes.

Honey was living her dream as she always had once she hit New York. She had dated a little here and there before Jared, but nothing serious, so when Kent entered the picture, her guard was down. They cared for each other over there. They iced each other's pain and rubbed their aches, and they had a connection she shared with no one else in the world—dancing and the love of it, how it transformed her into another place and time where no one could find her, but Kent found her there and joined her, and it was great to have someone to share that space with.

Honey had other friends who were dancers, male and female, but the chemistry between her and Kent could be seen and felt but couldn't be verbalized. It was electric when he touched her. She felt it through her entire body. They could fall asleep on the couch or laying across the bed without being intimate, but once they returned to the States and their respective homes, Honey longed for him. She missed his friendship. They talked on the phone frequently, and she shared everything with him that went on in her life as he did her. Eventually, the calls became daily, and when one didn't hear from the other, it was upsetting to their daily flow.

Jared was a very secure man. Their friendship didn't bother him, and he trusted her. She had never given him a reason not to, but he did sometimes want that same connection. It wasn't until he saw them together that he knew if he didn't put a stop to it, eventually something would happen. Kent got a job in New York, and it was a nine-month dance contract, and though he knew other people in New York, Honey was his main point of contact and who he spent his free time with.

One night, Honey was talking to Kent on the phone, and Jared listened to the laughter and the inside jokes they shared and stories from Europe and common interest and common people, and he told Honey he wasn't comfortable with the amount of time she invested in her relationship with Kent. She blew it off because there was nothing going on, but he was dead serious.

"There's nothing going on with us. You can't be serious," Honey protested almost laughingly.

"I'm serious, Honey. It's not you, but have you ever thought about what may be going through his mind, especially being single? I'm just not comfortable with the amount of time you guys spend together on the phone, and it needs to cut way down if not stop completely. I mean he's a man and I'm a man, and I know how men can think at times."

"Wait. What? Are you trying to tell me you don't want me to be friends with Kent?"

"You can make your own decisions. I can't make you do anything, but I am telling you how I feel, and I'd think that should count for something." He turned and walked out the door.
Honey sat there before calling Kent to tell him what had transpired, but she wasn't ready or willing to give him up. He was a piece of happiness she enjoyed. On the other hand, she understood where Jared was coming from and made an attempt to scale back, unsuccessfully.

Jared was leaving his office one day and was headed to meet a client when he spotted Kent and Honey having an early dinner. They looked like a couple. He saw the way they looked at each other. There was a forbidden flirtation between them. He called his client apologetically, rescheduling their meeting due to a family emergency. He walked over.

"Hey, baby," Honey said, slightly startled when he walked up.

"Hey, Jared man. What's up? Pull up a chair." Kent extended his hand for a shake.

They were sitting outside.

"Are you hungry, baby? We just ordered, so it's not too late to get something."

"Sure," he said, being as pleasant and nonthreatening as he could, but he watched them finish each other's sentences and how she touched his arm when they bantered back and forth. It was as if he was an intruder. They included him in the conversation, but it was almost as if it was to not be rude.

Honey hoped Jared being there with them would show him there was nothing there, but it was quite the opposite. It fueled the thoughts he already entertained.

The more time she spent with Kent, she realized she shared something that was missing with Jared. Intimacy. Passion. Both without sex. Her and Jared's sex life was good, and they got along well, but she wanted that along with whatever this was she had with Kent. When Jared finally put his foot down, asking her to completely give up her friendship with Kent, she wasn't willing to. She wouldn't let him dictate what she could and couldn't do. First, she would give into this, then the next thing you know she'd have her father on her hands. That was a far reach, and she knew how silly it was, but the bottom line was she wasn't doing it. She was never going to allow a man to control her life the way Josephine allowed Jim to control hers.

Jared told her he didn't want to give her an ultimatum, but if she preferred his friendship to their relationship then that was what it would be. She got all in a huff and went to her friend Cecily's apartment, and Cecily talked some sense into her. Why would she give up Jared as good as he was to her and the lifestyle he provided for her? She would be crazy to walk away from it all and have to live on her dancer's salary, especially as she was getting older and lived in New York.

"Do you think you may just want to have sex with him and get it out the way? Maybe it's the sexual tension that has you so intrigued. Probably once you do, you'll see that's all it is. You and Jared have something real that you two have been building for years. Are you willing to throw that away on 'chemistry' and 'connection'?" Cecily gave her the air quotes. "You better stop and think, girl."

Three glasses of wine later, she saw her point—not the having sex with Kent part because she knew that would only complicate things and more than likely tie her to him even more, especially if they were as sexually compatible as they were in all the other areas of their lives. She wasn't willing to risk it. Cecily was right. She was building a life with Jared that looked good on more than just paper.

"Let me get this over with." She looked over at Cecily, let out a long sigh, grunted and grabbed the phone to call Kent. She dialed the number and hung up four times before actually letting it ring through.

"This is horrible, Cece, I don't want to give him up. I want things to stay like they are. I want them both. I mean, men have been having their cake and eating it to for centuries," she whined. "Well, I want mine too."

"Girl, if you don't stop being foolish and call that man and tell him goodbye, you're going to lose your real man." Cecily shook her head. "But that's on you. Just don't come crying to me this time next year when you wish you had made a different decision because Jared has made it clear it isn't going down, and he's kicking you to the curb if you think you're 'bout to play him like that." She laughed a little but was dead serious.

"Okay! Man." She dialed again, and Kent picked up. "*Ummm, heyyyy. Ummm, so ummm…*"

"What's wrong? Spit it out." He laughed.

Honey cleared her throat. "See, the thing is, Jared is really serious about me not continuing in this friendship with you, and for the sake of my relationship, not that I want to, I *ummm* am not going to be able to stay in touch. I mean, I love you. You have become my closest friend, which is probably the problem, you know?"

"Okay, *ummm,* wow. Well, I definitely understand, and I am not here to step on anyone's toes or wreck any relationships, but I will have to say I am going to miss you, but I respect your decision."

"So just like that, that's it?"

"I mean what do you want me to say? This is you and Jared's decision not mine. I guess you two are makin' the rules. I'm just following them. You can't be mad at that. You called me. I didn't call you to end our friendship."

Honey was a little irritated. She wanted him to be a little resistant. She didn't want him to bow out so easily, but he did, and that broke her heart just a little. "Well, okay then. I guess that's it. I hope you get everything you want in life, Kent. You're an amazing man."

"Yeah, you too. I love you, Honey," he blurted and quickly hung up the phone.

She looked down at the phone. "He hung up, just like that." She looked over at Cecily. "He said he loved me and hung up. What am I supposed to do with that?"

"Nothing. Go home to your man."

Nothing is as easy as that. The very next day after rehearsal, she went to call Kent to tell him about something that happened with Becca, another dancer, then she realized what she was doing and hung up. It was hard. She tried to share some of the stories with Jared she would normally share with Kent, but it just wasn't the same. She shared her days and stories with Jared before Kent came along, and there was never an issue. He actively listened, remembered who people were and gave feedback, but having shared what she had with Kent, it just wasn't the same. Before she knew it, she was talking to Kent and even meeting him behind Jared's back.

Kent was never really quite comfortable with it, but he missed Honey, their friendship and emotional connection. He would date other women here and there but they never measured up, especially when he compared them to Honey.

When the dance contract ended, he decided to stay in New York, and this was just a disaster waiting to happen. Who were they fooling? They knew something was there, but they refused to act on it, and this was their justification for remaining in the forbidden friendship.

That year, they had both auditioned for a touring dance company, and both were picked up, which meant they would be on the road for three months initially, but if all went well, the tour was likely to be extended. She was so excited, and when she told Jared, who had no idea Kent was going along for the ride, he was excited for her as he always was. He supported everything she was and desired to be. The tour was starting on the West Coast in San Francisco and would hit sixteen major cities in that three months.

Honey talked to Jared every morning and every night, and never once mentioned anything about Kent. She lived in her fantasy of having it all—until Houston. Jared flew out to surprise her. He was going to stay for two days because she would have one day off before they left for the next city. She and Kent along with a few other dancers from the company were in her room when there was a knock. Honey's roommate went to open the door and to Jared's surprise there was Honey siting on the couch with her feet in Kent's lap being rubbed. When Honey saw Jared she jumped up.

"Heyyy, baby," she said nervously. "What are you doing here? I didn't know you were coming."

Kent just sat there and looked on.

"Clearly," Jared said and left.

Honey chased after him. "Wait. Wait." She attempted to keep up with him. "I can explain."

"Can you, Honey? The funny thing is there shouldn't ever be anything going on that needs an explanation. I'm done. When you get off tour, we can deal with how to end this. You're not going to make a fool of me. I trusted—no, no, I trust you," he said angrily, "and this is how you return my trust."

"Jared, there's nothing going on."

"Honey, at this point it doesn't even matter. You are where you want to be, so go be there. You don't have to worry about hiding Kent from me, which is obviously what you were doing. Not only are you still in contact with him after you told me you weren't. I come to surprise you because I'm at home missing you so much, man— missing you crazy like—and you're here getting foot rubs by someone you're no longer in contact with. *Hmmm.* How the hell does that happen, Honey?"

Jared had never cursed at her. He had never really raised his voice at her. He was angry, but she could tell he was hurt more than anything, and she felt it. She caused this, and now she was so sorry.

"I'm sorry, baby. I knew if I told you he was going to be on the tour you wouldn't want me to come, and this is my life. Dancing is my life, Jared."

"It's cool. I thought I was part of this life of yours, and I thought honesty and integrity were a part of your—no, our—life. Guess I was wrong about both."

He turned and walked away as she called out to him, but he was done. There was nothing he wanted to hear at that point.

She made her way back to the room where the atmosphere had completely changed.

"He left?" Kent questioned. She nodded. "Are you okay?" She shook her head. "Is there anything I can do?" She nodded. "What is it? What can I do?"

"Leave."

So he did. It was funny how they were inseparable for over a year, and now she didn't even want to look at him. She wanted to blame him, but it wasn't his fault. It was her own, and she knew it. She called Cecily to tell her what had happened. As much as she wanted to say "I told you so," she resisted. Instead she comforted her friend and assured her it was going to work out and that she and Jared were meant for each other.

"We can fix this. I promise. Jared loves you, Honey. You just have to love him back the way he deserves to be loved. I'm here for you."

She lay in the bed stewing in her mess all night. She called Jared, but he didn't answer. She only called once because she felt like if she kept calling it would make her look guilty, and though she was wrong, she didn't really do anything other than kinda break his trust, she thought.

She knew if she had any hope of salvaging the relationship, she had to go home. Now not only was she giving up one thing she loved, Kent, but now her dancing was being compromised. She went to the production manager of the show that next morning explaining she had a family emergency and needed to leave the tour. She had a good reputation and knew this would hurt her but prayed her prior track record would cover her.

She packed her things and booked a flight home. She debated if she should even say goodbye to Kent. She was angry with him because she didn't want to be angry with herself. As she was packing, there was a knock, and she knew it was probably him. Maybe she should just go cold turkey she thought and sneak out and never look back, but he deserved more than that. Though she knew this, she couldn't bring herself to go to the door. She plopped down on the bed after she'd finished gathering her things and sobbed. After she got her much-needed cry out, the inner pep talk began.

"You can do this. He loves you. You guys can work this out. You got this." The self-talk continued as she grabbed her bag and opened the door. Startled by Kent sitting in the hallway on the floor across from the room, she jumped. "You scared me."

"So, it's like that? You're just going to sneak out without so much as a bye or I never want to see you again or anything? I thought we were better than that."

"I'm just confused, Kent. I just hurt the man who's been there for me, who supports me in everything I do, and I betrayed him."

"So again, you're just going to leave like I mean nothing? I mean I'm all good until you have to make a choice, right? You called me back into your life. You said you missed me, remember? I respected your decision when you tried to end our friendship because at least you talked to me and let me know what was going on. But this right here, I can't respect. You're skulking off like a New York City rat."

She let her suitcase go and walked over to him. "It's not like that, and you know it. I just don't know what to do. I love you, Kent." She grabbed his face and looked him in his eyes. "But I can't lose Jared. I just can't."

"Okay then, that's what you say. You don't just get to leave, man. You don't just get to leave."

She hugged him tighter than anyone she had ever hugged in her entire life. "I'm sorry."

"Never be sorry. I'm not." He looked at the tears in her eyes, not really knowing if they were for him or for Jared as she let go.

She grabbed her suitcase handle and headed down the hall. She was getting ready to turn the corner, and as she took one final glance back, he was still there watching. He was watching the woman he had slowly and unconsciously fallen in love with walk out of his life as haphazardly as she had walked in. She thought, *I should have never looked back.* She quickly pranced back toward him. She looked at him, grabbed one hand while placing the other on his cheek, and she lightly allowed her lips to brush his. He returned the gesture with a passionate goodbye kiss that sent sparks flying and completely confirmed the chemistry that was there all along. They kissed and stopped and kissed again, transcending into a place neither of them had known but were glad to finally be there, until finally she pulled away, turned and left, this time not looking back.

Making her way to the airport, the anxiety filled her the entire cab ride. Rehearsing the various ways this scenario could play out, she hoped for the best. Remembering she had Kent to fall back on if Jared really didn't take her back was somehow not as comforting as she thought it might be. She boarded her flight and headed home to win her man back. When she arrived, he wasn't there. He had stayed in Houston and wouldn't be arriving until the following day as scheduled, which she didn't know until she finally called from the house phone and he answered.

"What are you doing home?"

"Because I'm not willing to lose the one thing that means more than anything to me. I'm so sorry, baby. I'll never give you a reason not to trust me ever again. I don't know what I was thinking. I just I don't know. I was just being silly I guess. It seemed exciting to have a new person to share my life with that I clicked with, and I guess I felt like it made our life seem a little boring and predictable. I am getting older, and I just don't know… There is really no excuse. I just want to fix this. I realized when you walked away from me you're all I need. I felt like I was dying on the inside. I just can't imagine my life without you."

"But it took you losing me to know how good we have it?" He was puzzled. "I never look for anything exciting and new because after all this time, you still excite me. I look forward to seeing you every morning, every night and enjoy of the predictable and sometimes mundane things in between. You have and always will be enough for me. I just wish I was the same for you."

"I know it's not right, and it's definitely not fair to you, but I just want to be honest. I don't want to start over without being completely honest, Jared, and you're enough. You are," she pleaded with him. "I'm so sorry I took what we have for granted—that I took you for granted. Please don't leave me. I love you."

He was overwhelmed with her raw vulnerability, which he only seemed to see when she danced, and he knew he couldn't let her go. He never really had any intention. He thought she wanted out, and he wasn't going to stand in her way, but now he saw she didn't, that she just made a mistake, and it was one he was ready to forgive. Just as Honey couldn't imagine herself without Jared, he couldn't imagine his life without her. Of course he could always find someone else with whom to share his life, but no one would ever be Honey.

He didn't let on all would be forgiven that easily. He explained they could talk about it more when he returned home.

Honey waited impatiently for him to arrive home. She tossed and turned all night. When she finally heard his keys in the door, she jumped up and ran toward the door. She barely allowed him space to step inside before putting her arms around his neck and beginning her apology once again.

He stepped back, pulled her up to him, and kissed her long and hard as if for the very first time.

"I'm sorry," she said.

"I don't want to hear I'm sorry again. It's over, okay? We're okay," he said. "Now, what about the tour?"

"What about it? I realized last night there's nothing that's ever going to come before you again—I mean nothing, not even dancing. I messed up, and whatever I have to do to make it right, I'm going to do it and not begrudgingly. It's because I want to because I love you."

Jared was still a little angry on the inside, but he knew it was his ego more than anything but he also knew Honey, and he knew she meant exactly what she said, but he didn't want her giving up her dreams for him and waking up one day bitter and resentful. No thank you. That night, the lovemaking was sweeter than it had ever been, and the next day over breakfast, as they talked, she began to realize what she was really saying she was giving up. She began to cry, which helped create the brainstorming idea behind the birth of Flight.

She never talked to Kent after that but heard through dance colleagues he had moved to London. She was happy for him. He was an amazing dancer, but she had to admit sometimes she missed him and the friendship they shared but never enough to reach out and definitely not enough to risk losing Jared.

Honey was well known and well liked in her community. As Diane had developed her passion for helping women, Honey, once grounded, had developed a sense of responsibility to young girls, especially underprivileged girls who may want to dance, but never be able to afford it or have the opportunity to be exposed. In addition to Flight, she developed a nonprofit program that served the community, and the girls she taught loved her. She cared about them, not just their dancing abilities. She was mother to some, big sister to others and auntie to yet others, and she loved every moment of seeing the possibilities that hope brings.

Flight was just as successful of a business as she had been a dancer and she was full. She couldn't have asked for a better life, and though it started out a little shaky, God had not let her down in the end, and she was thankful. Some of the turmoil she had gone through developed the compassion she was able to express to the young girls she mentored, and she always said if that's what it took for her to become who she was, it was worth it.

Life Has a Way of Breaking Us

Diane and June were in the kitchen talking about a bunch of nothing until June spoke on her epiphany.

"What do you think about me moving to Atlanta?" June looked over at Diane waiting to see her facial response.

"Wait, what?" Diane said excitedly, "Are you serious?

"I mean you know there is so much I love about California, but I miss being near family. California seemed to be a million miles away. At least all you guys are on the same side of the country. L.A. is getting more expensive by the day, and the traffic is getting worse. Maybe it's time for a change."

"How long have you been thinking about this?"

"Not long at all. Being here and being with you guys was the push I think I needed to make the decision."

"I'm seriously thinking about it if you let me stay with you while I look for a new job, which shouldn't be hard for a nurse, and then a place."

"You're serious?" Diane stopped midcut into the pie she was preparing for herself and looked at June.

"Yes. Yes, now that I've said it aloud. I'm actually pretty serious. I know I have a pretty good life in California, and I have my friends and everything, but I think I'm ready for a change, and Atlanta is growing. You seem to like it there a lot. I mean, I need to pray about it of course and make sure it's what the Lord is saying, but I feel like it might be the right time."

Diane let out a sigh. "I'm good with you coming, June. You know I'd love to have my sister there with me—shoot, both my sisters if we could get Honey and Jared on board." She laughed. "But seriously, don't get on that God stuff with me, and you are more than welcome."

"You kill me calling it God stuff, like God hasn't kept you—us—from what we deserve."

"What's that supposed to mean?" Diane looked at her sternly.

"You know exactly what it means. God has been good to us… Well, let me stop speaking for you. God has been good to me. If you only knew some of the trauma I've been through—far worse than some of the stuff we had to go through growing up—and I still have my sanity. I'm not bitter. I'm whole and happy. Nothing but the grace of God could have done that for me."

June thought back to being molested by Jim and watching him beat their mother and being helpless, to the wild life she lived the first few years in California and how hard it was to get clean, go to nursing school and stay clean in a city that offered her everything for the price of her soul, and she undoubtedly believed it was only God in his love and grace and mercy that allowed her to be standing there today.

"Well, God hasn't been so good to me okay, June? He just hasn't. My life has been a glass full of trauma from day one. Every time I yell bottoms up and gulp down what I think is the last of the trauma, my glass somehow is refilled each time more bitter than the last, and what do I do? I down it and let it burn as I swallow whatever happens to be in the glass at that time. I'm tired, June, and honestly, if there is a God, where is he? Why has he allowed my life to be one bitter pill after the next?"

"Why, because your marriage didn't work? Which is still baffling to us all. You guys seemed so happy and so in love. What really happened? Did he cheat on you or something?" June asked.

"Oh my God. Why does it always have to be infidelity that ends a marriage?"

"I'm just asking since you've never said, and it just doesn't make any sense."

"June, sometimes just because you're in love with someone and they seemingly love you, too, doesn't mean they're for you. It doesn't mean it's meant to be. That's the hard part about love. It doesn't guarantee it all works out the way you want it to in the end. But what it will guarantee, I can assure you, is a little heartache and sometimes a whole lot of heartache. You know that saying if you love someone set them free?" June nodded. "Okay, well sometimes you have to do what's best for someone else. That's what true love is. It's unselfish."

"That's exactly what Christ's love did for us. He didn't deserve to die on the cross, to drink from the bitter cup, but he did it for me, for you—for us—but I won't get into that, and even though I know the saying, it does also say something about if they were meant for you, they come back or something like that? Besides, how could you not be good for anyone? You're amazing, one of the most amazing women I know. You're so accomplished and do so much for the people around you. I'm so confused."

"Me too." Diane stared off. "But life has a way of breaking us and disappointing us, and smart people know when to throw in the towel in the areas they have no control over and focus on the areas they do.

"You need to remember who God is, Diane, and you need to know that no matter how it looks, he's there. You just need to call on him. Sooo, I'm gonna leave it right there."

"Please do because I don't know where God was when that bastard was tormenting us. I've called out to God so many times, yet there I always stand broken and alone."

"Do you ever think about him, you know, like what was wrong with him?" June leaned back as if really trying to figure out the answer to her own question.

"Not one day," Diane said very matter of factly. "Not one day. I was happy he was gone then, and I'm still happy about it. I never wonder what was wrong with him. I just wonder when what he did will stop waking me up some nights."

"Well, what about Richard? Do you ever still think about him or wonder what he's doing? Wait, you guys aren't still in touch, are you?"

"Nope, for the best."

"For the best, huh?"

"Yep."

"According to who? You or him?"

"What difference does it make now?"

"You'll only know if you call him."

"Well, that's not going to happen, sooo let's just move on."

"But you're not moving on. You don't even date, and it's been almost five years, Diane. I mean really, come on. If you weren't still in love with him, you would at least have dated someone—anyone. Clearly, it's not because you're trying to live right before God or anything." June let out a small laugh. "If you're still breathing, it's never too late—unless your battery-operated boyfriend is all the man you need."

"I don't share your view of love, June. Forgive me. I love you, I love family, and I love community. I'll do whatever is necessary to help people who've been wronged, who justice and law don't stand up for. This leaves me no room to love a mere man. Why would I do that to myself? Why would I give someone power over me?"

"Diane, you just don't get it. It's not about giving up power, it's about sharing life."

"Well, forgive me if I don't want to share in the life of Jim and Josephine or June and Charlie, which, by your own admission, was a clear mess. Talking about giving up power."

"You're just afraid because you don't trust God."

Diane laughed feverishly. "Trust God. Did you say trust God? The same God that Momma trusted her whole life and that Jim proclaimed to be led by? That same God? The one who didn't keep us safe and didn't protect us?" Diane stood and began to pace. "You're right, June. I don't want any parts of that God."

"You need to remember that same God kept you out of jail," June interjected.

She wanted to believe, but how could she, after all her family had experienced at the hands of their own father and no one intervened but her? No heavenly hand came down and rescued them. He, if he is there, sat up there in heaven and just watched. He just watched, and Diane had never forgiven him for just watching. She sat back down in complete silence, remembering how she stepped in and ended things when God wouldn't like it was yesterday.

"I'm listening to you, but I'm not believing you. First of all, who doesn't believe in God? You sound ridiculous. Second of all, I know you loved and still love Richard. I don't care what you say. Now you need to stop and just get real with yourself. Life is too short. Who are you putting on a front for? There's nothing wrong with love, and being in love, as long as it's with the right person, it's phenomenal. Momma loved the wrong person. That doesn't have to be you. Heck, I loved the wrong person, but it's not making me give up on love and knowing the right person is out there. Shoot, maybe he's in Atlanta." She laughed and took a sip of her soda.

"Yeah, but you just don't know what we've been through and what I put him through." She slumped down. "You know how you can always see things clearer after you've messed them up? There's no way he could possibly want me, especially after all this time."

"But if he still loves you and is still single…" June sang.

"That's just it. First of all, who knows if he's still single, and second of all, the way things ended, he probably never wants to even hear my name, let alone my voice."

"The thing is, you don't want to die never knowing. Where is the Diane Unafraid, huh? Where's my real sister? You're an imposter because my real sister isn't afraid of anything. My sister would literally kill for me."

They both stopped for a moment to reflect on the weight of the statement that just came from June's mouth. It's funny the things we become afraid of when we go through this obstacle course we call life.

"Get the phone. Let's find out," June said, hopeful.

"What the hell? Let me get the house phone I don't want to use my minutes." Diane figured she had been through so many hurts and losses in her life. How much damage could one more cause? Didn't she have a right to find out, or was it best not knowing?

She dialed the number and waited and waited and waited, then hung up.

"Well," June said anxiously, "why did you hang up?"

"Because there was no answer."

"Why didn't you leave a message?"

"I don't know. I just couldn't."

"Oh my God, this is ridiculous. Call back," June said forcefully, "and leave a message." Picking up the phone, she pushed it into Diane's hand. "Don't be a wimp. Just do it."

"Fine." She snatched the phone and called back. "It's still ringing." She looked over at June.

"Hello," a voice answered.

Diane was silent. "Is it still ringing?" June asked anxiously.

"Who is this?"

She hung up right in his face.

"Did you really just hang up again? The point was to leave a message. What is wrong with you? You stand up to tough judges and deal with social issues every day, and you're afraid of a voicemail. This is utterly ridiculous. I'm ashamed to be your sister right now."

"He answered, and I panicked. I was ready to leave a message. I thought he wasn't there, and then he answered." Her voice got faster, and her heart raced as she stood and paced the floor. Just then the phone rang.

"It's him." Diane looked at the caller ID.

"Well, answer it." June pushed her.

"I can't."

"Lord, girl, give me the phone." June snatched it. "Hello."

"*Ummm,* yeah. Who's calling me from this number?"

"Hi, Richard. This is June, Diane's sister. How are you?"

"Hey, June. How have you been? Is everything okay with Diane? She is okay, isn't she?" She could sense the concern in his voice.

"Oh, no, nothing like that. She's fine, just being a bit silly right now for lack of a better term."

"Silly?" he repeated. "What do you mean?"

June went on to explain what had just transpired with the calling of his number and Diane being afraid to leave a message as if she were twelve. He chuckled a bit before saying if she was okay, there was nothing really they had to talk about. June insisted there was, but he said no thanks. He couldn't deal with Diane's type of crazy, that it had taken him a long time to move forward, and now that he had, he couldn't allow himself to revisit the most painful part of his life.

"It was good hearing from you, June. Take care." Then there was dead silence from the disconnected call.

"I knew it. See, June. I knew it. You just had to butt in. I can't believe I let you talk me into this." She left, slamming the door behind her.

"Don't you even want to know what he said?" she yelled. The next thing she heard was Diane pulling out of the driveway, tires screeching and all. *Maybe I should have just let it go,* June thought, but she really wanted Diane to be happy, and she knew Richard made her happy—at least at some point in life he did.

The real issue was the brokenness that needed so desperately to be healed in them all. Josephine ready to die, Diane afraid of love, June facing the fear of not falling back into her old lifestyle and poor little Honey loving Jared yet still some days feeling as if she is missing out on something, but just what she didn't know.

As Diane drove through the familiar streets, the tears were like lava oozing from a volcano. She didn't even try to stop them. It had been so long since she had cried, she almost forgot she knew how. Somehow, it felt good and miserable at the same time. Her heart hurt physically, and the lava tears were now soaking her t-shirt, and her vision was so blurred she had to pull over. She sat there looking around remembering her childhood. It seemed like it was so bad, but there were good times too. Everything wasn't as bad as it seemed, was it? She wondered why her family couldn't have been normal. But exactly what was normal, and by whose standards? All she knew was the things that transpired in that house shouldn't be a part of anyone's upbringing or life for that matter.

She sat there about forty minutes before she could pull herself together enough to decide to get ice cream to make her feel better. There was nothing like ice cream to soothe the soul, mend a heart and melt all one's troubles away.

Meanwhile seven hundred miles away, Richard wondered what that phone call was about. He had desperately tried to close that chapter of his life, but the truth was he still loved and missed Diane. His heart had been broken, and he tried to move on, but no one was her. He came close once, but as perfect as Vanessa was, she wasn't perfect for him. He made a go of it with her for nearly two years, but when it came down to it, he just couldn't do it, especially once she began talking about marriage and wondering where the relationship was headed. She didn't pressure him, but at the same time, she made it perfectly clear if that wasn't the direction the relationship was headed, she had to cut her losses because she had no time to be wasting at her age. She knew she was a valuable asset to complement any man in a relationship, and she also knew she wanted to be a wife not a girlfriend and that almost two years should have been long enough for him to see her value and determine what to do with it.

Needless to say, though he believed she was a beautiful, educated and self-sufficient woman who any man would be crazy not to have, just call him crazy—crazy for Diane and the possibility of what he had with her to exist once again. But it never did, and he was mad at himself for not knowing how to move forward. He wasn't bitter but still slightly angry with the way the marriage ended. Mainly because he just couldn't understand how she could just walk away. He was invested, with or without children. Adopting or birthing, he was committed, and she said she was only thinking about his feelings, but he began to realize it wasn't for him. It was for her—her fears, her shortcomings and not wanting to face the reality of what life had dealt her. She couldn't face not having the ability to control her world.

Richard didn't know about the things she had lived through, the choices that made her into the person she had become. She loved at a distance, always with one toe out the door, always in position to not be hurt, and that was no way to live. The funny thing is he understood it enough to love her through it—or maybe in spite of it—but just not enough to make her stay. He couldn't help but wonder why she was calling. He kind of started kicking himself a little for not hearing June out. He was guarded, he was a man, and he wasn't going to allow himself to be vulnerable again.

When It All Comes Out

The night before they all were to head back to their separate lives, Josephine planned a big dinner. The girls helped out in the kitchen. They talked and laughed. Josephine sang as she often did when she cooked, and nothing could touch them in this bubble of safety they created when they were together.

"Is your son coming over?" Diane threw a disapproving look to her mother.

"Don't start, Diane. You know he's coming over. It's your last night here."

"But he doesn't even like us," Honey exclaimed.

Josephine would never allow them to speak badly of their brother if he wasn't there to defend himself. That was her son no matter what. For as many bad qualities as he had, he had some good ones as well. She believed in family and wanted them to be close with him as they were with one another, but he was so very different from them. His bond and allegiance were to Jim. He would let the girls in but only so far. Deep down, he loved them but wasn't taught to express that love.

"You may not understand your brother, but everyone has redeeming qualities. No one is perfect, not one of you, so I won't stand here and listen to you belittle your brother. You're all each other has, and you need to start acting like it."

They just couldn't understand how she could take up for him the way he treated her and talked to her at times. He would do things for her financially, but more so just to say he did or to boast about it to make himself look like a good son, much like Jim.

"One day if you ever have children of your own, you'll understand. Children are the most precious blessing, and you protect them at all cost, so until then hush." She went on humming a little tune.

"Maybe some of us can't have children," Diane mumbled under her breath.

"What was that?" Josephine stopped. "Are you getting smart with me under your breath?"

"No, Momma, I wasn't."

"Well, what did you say, Diane?"

"Nothing."

"Well, it couldn't have been nothing. It was in you enough that you couldn't hold, but you weren't bold enough to say it. So go ahead, say it. What's on your mind?"

Diane stopped chopping the onions and looked down at the floor, taking a deep breath. "I said maybe, just maybe some of us can't have children. I guess that means I'll never know what it's like to have the 'most precious blessing.'" She used air quotes.

Everyone paused, and the room was quiet.

"Oh, Diane, I am…" Josephine said, but before she could get it out, Diane cut her off.

"Please, everyone, keep doing what you're doing. It's not a big deal. I don't need your pity."

But it was a big deal. It is one thing if you have no desire to have children. There's nothing wrong with that, but when you try so hard and keep coming up short, it's actually not okay. No one really knew what to say to this bombshell that was just unloaded right in the middle of the kitchen floor.

Diane wasn't an emotional person, but she felt the tears welling up in her eyes, and she knew she needed to make a mad dash. As she went to exit the kitchen, June caught her by the hand.

"You've gotta stop running at some point, sister."

But she wasn't ready to stop because stopping meant she had to deal with how she had handled her life from that fateful night to her divorce to every other bad decision she had made thus far. She pulled away from June.

"I'm fine. It's not a big deal." She ran upstairs to the bathroom.

"Did you know about this?" Josephine questioned the girls.

But they didn't. No one in their family knew, and that's how she thought it should be.

Diane the protector never wanted anyone feeling sorry for her or taking care of her. That was her job to take care of her family; friends, which were few; and the community around her. They each looked back and forth to one another determining who would go after her. Finally, after the long, silent looks, June volunteered.

What was it? June thought as she walked up the stairs to locate Diane. First, she had to go bringing up Richard and opening that can of worms, and now their mother had opened another can. She was contemplating what approach to take with each step. Where could she start without having any idea what was going on. After all, what did she mean by "couldn't have"? What did that mean? She questioned herself repeatedly, and did she really want to wake the sleeping giant? Whether she did or not, she had to. Honey and Josephine were waiting for answers below.

She heard the running water in the bathroom and knocked.

"Hey. What's going on? I would ask if you're okay, but clearly you're not. So what's up? Let's have it."

"It's nothing. I just need a minute."

"Girl, stop. I'm not about to do this BS with you. You only need a minute when you need to recover from something. So what is it? And for God's sake, come out the dang bathroom. I'm not doing this with you today."

Diane stood resting her hands on the sink, looking at herself in the mirror, wondering how it came to this and kicking herself for even making the comment in the first place. How would she explain not trusting them with the hardest time of her life when they had helped her through the most scariest, life-changing time? They kept the secrets no one should ever be asked to keep, and they stood strong. Maybe she didn't want to burden them with anything else.

She was a hard person to figure out. There was the strong advocate fighting for all that was true and right determined to fix the wrongs even if it was only one wrong at a time. The girl no one saw or even knew about—the scared, wounded and violated little girl who was never saved, the little girl who couldn't save herself but was determined to save her sister. No one knew that deep down she wanted to be saved, She wanted to not be strong. She wanted to rest, but the type of rest she needed eluded her. She looked again, sighed and grabbed a fresh cloth from the bathroom cabinet to wash her face.

"Just give me another minute, June, and I'll be down."

"Yeah, no. How about I just wait?"

June was sitting on the floor at the door. When the handle began to turn, she jumped up. As soon as Diane saw her, she broke down before June could even say anything. "So what version of being alright would this be?" She hugged her and shook her head.

"What's going on, Diane?"

"Huh?" Diane sighed. "June, you wouldn't understand."

"Oh, I wouldn't? Girl, you just don't know how much I do understand. You think you're the only one who has hurts and pain they try to bury? Well, you're not, and shutting us out isn't going to help you."

She grabbed Diane's hand, pulling her toward the stairs. "Momma made coffee."

"Coffee? I need a drink." Diane let out a half-hearted chuckle. "Can I get some liquor in mine? I'm serious.'

"Well, good thing it's still early so we can deal with this before your brother gets here."

"That's your brother. I don't claim that fool. When people ask if I have siblings, I say yes, two sisters," Diane said, looking over at June.

They both laughed hysterically even though it wasn't that funny. There needed to be something to cut the heaviness in the air.

Diane and June sat in the living room, the famous meeting spot. Honey hollered from the kitchen, "Y'all want some Blueberry Buckle from this morning."

"I do!" June blurted before Honey could barely finish the question. She looked over at Diane. "Girl, eat some Buckle."

They laughed again feverishly and once again for no real reason, but it felt good. Diane was actually beginning to feel light, a feeling she was unfamiliar with. How can anyone carrying such burdens all the time ever be light?

As June and Josephine arrived with the coffee and Buckle, it was time to set all this nonsense aside and get down to the meat of the situation, as Josephine often said.

"Okay, girls." She sat down, letting out a huge sigh, not partaking in the treats. Each girl, however, immediately reaching for their liquid strength. "Now what exactly is going on, Diane? And you two are not off the hook. I know one of you knew something. First, you run out of here yesterday like a bat out of hell and then today you talk about not having children and go running off upstairs. Now what in the devil is the meaning of it all? I want answers. Real answers, I mean it now." She sat back and looked at Diane who was looking down into her mug.

"Everything isn't that simple, Momma."

"Everything except the things you make hard," Josephine replied.

"Fine!" She stood, rocking back and forth almost in a small pacing four step. She cleared her throat looking between the three of their faces, before clearing her throat again. "Okay, well it's not that big of a deal now. But—" She cleared her throat again.

"Oh for goodness' sake," Honey pushed, "just spit it out already."

"Stop being so immature, Honey. Give your sister a minute," Josephine scolded her.

"Okay, so you know how I told you things just didn't work out with me and Richard?" They all nodded. "Okay, well the truth is I left him."

"What?" Josephine looked shocked.

"I mean, I know I said we just had some things we couldn't resolve and thought it would be better to just throw in the towel before it got bad, but the truth is, well, he begged me not to do it, but I couldn't. I couldn't allow him to stay with me knowing I could never give him the one thing he desperately wanted: children."

"Well, did he say he only wanted to stay married to you if you could have kids?" June asked.

Simultaneously, Honey questioned why they didn't just adopt, and Josephine asked how she even knew she couldn't have children or if it was just something the doctors told her. She didn't trust doctors as far as she could see them.

"Look, it really doesn't matter at this point. It's over and done. He's moved on with his life."

"Is he married to someone else?"

"I don't know, Honey. I just don't know. But if he is, good for him. He deserves to be happy."

"But you guys seemed so happy. He was happy, Diane. Sometimes you're so bullheaded, just like your father that you can't see what's good for you, even when it's right in your face." Josephine let out an exhausted sigh.

"Wow, Momma, that was low." Diane stood to walk out.

"Nope. Nope. Sit down. Nobody's running today. You girls been runnin' too long—your whole adult lives—and I know part of it's my fault. I know that, but I had to make peace with my decisions, and it's time you did too. If not, life will live you when you should be livin' it."

Diane turned and slumped hard in the chair with an attitude. As much as she wanted to leave, she dared not be disrespectful, so she did as she was told.

"I know the three of you probably secretly blame me for the way you are when it comes to men. Don't know if you are comin' or goin', wanting to love but too scared. Wanna have the kind of love you see in the movies. I wanted that too. Shoot, I had it for a while, but old Jim began to change. Nothing was ever good enough. He was battling demons you girls would never understand. Heck, I didn't understand them, some of them myself, but I was his wife."

"No, you were his punching bag, Momma." Diane's eyes began to fill with tears once again, and this time it made her angry. Jim was dead and gone, and still they weren't free.

"During those times, it wasn't like it is today. Where was I going to go with four babies looking up at me? How was I gonna take care of you and raise you at the same time? It couldn't be done. It just couldn't. But that's neither here nor there now."

They all just sat there with their thoughts, each of them hating Jim for a different reason yet somehow oddly the same. Diane had never shared with anyone what Jim had done to her, and neither did June. No one knew Jim had molested June on more than one occasion, but she thought if she didn't do it, he would take it out on Josephine, and she had already endured so much under the tyrannical brut. The beatings, the verbal abuse, the mental and emotional abuse, it never seemed to end.

"Maybe you should just call Richard, Diane," Honey said.

"We tried that yesterday, which is the reason she peeled out of the driveway running over animals and small children," June said to Honey.

"Shut up." Diane threw a pillow at her.

She began to explain the saga of the three miscarriages and how she just couldn't go through it again. It was the happiest and the worst time of her life all mushed together.

"You guys just don't know how hard it was. After the first miscarriage, I was so sure when I got pregnant again it couldn't possibly happen two times in row, and then bam, not only a second time, but a third."

"How could we know if you didn't let us in? I can't believe you went through all that alone. I'm so sorry, Diane." Honey reached over and hugged her. "You know, I still think you should try with Richard. I mean, what could it hurt? It's only been a few years? You sound like you still want to be with him, but you were just scared of who and what you weren't.

Diane just sat there contemplating. If in fact he was single, which he probably wasn't, how would she even get him to take her call? To even hear her out? Underneath all the armor she had built for protection, at the heart of it, she really did want to be loved—and loved by Richard specifically. The things you think will replace the things you truly desire to have always let you down. Her work was powerful, the people she'd helped in her career and even in her personal life grateful. Whenever and if there was ever a need to be fulfilled for someone, there was never a question or doubt in her mind to give whatever it took to fill it.

Her mother used to always say, "You can't take it with you. We were designed to be a blessing to others," and though Diane always felt slighted in some way, due to her life's experience, she had the heart of a giver. Happiness was always a grasp away, and disappointment was clearly an inevitable theme of her life. Could this ever change, and was she willing to take the risk to bring change?

June was already devising a scheme to contact Richard. There had to be a way to fix this while Diane was actually feeling emotions, which was rare. Anything other than anger, that is. But she had a right to be angry with all she had been through. Unfortunately, her anger was getting her nowhere. It was the fuel that helped her fight for others, but it left her more broken by the day.

"What can we do? What can I do to help you, Diane honey? You girls mean everything to me, and I just want to see you happy."

"Nothing, Momma. There is nothing anyone can do. Life is sometimes just meant to work out for some and not for others."

"Diane, God has a plan for everyone's life. You just have to be willing to tune into God's frequency and get some clear direction. I mean it's admirable and all the things you do, but at the end of the day, what are you left with? My bed is empty, and I'm glad it's empty, and I've never had a desire to fill it after Jim was gone, but you, on the other hand, had—no, you can still have—something good. Don't be a fool then one day look back with regrets."

It was hard to hear, hard to be vulnerable, but Diane listened and nodded, but this whole looking weak thing was new to her, and she didn't like it. Not that being vulnerable makes a person look weak, but in her mind's eye, it did just that.

Good-bye Dinner

A s Jim Jr. and Charlene arrived with the children, it was bittersweet. This marked the end of a visit Josephine knew would come, but heavily resisted. She enjoyed having the girls home, in spite of the unexpected emotional turns.

Honey and Jim Jr. sat outside on the porch. Jim Jr. was sitting on the rail while Honey swung back and forth on the swing. She sighed as he looked off into the distance.

"You know, it wasn't all bad, I guess." Honey closed her eyes and let the cool breeze wash over her.

"What are you talking about?"

"You know, I'm just saying growing up was pretty bad. Don't get me wrong, but it wasn't all bad, like one hundred percent of the time. I was just thinking how you and I used to ride our bikes, and I would let you win so you wouldn't cry and how that time Mark Williams was being so mean to me, and as big as he was, you stood up for me and said no one was going to mess with your sister except you." She began to chuckle. "What happened to that boy?"

He sat there in thought for a minute. Normally something like that would have angered him, but this day he pondered the words in his heart before turning to Honey. "I don't really know, but I guess Daddy happened. Not making excuses, I just am who I am."

"Yeah, I guess, but you know you don't have to be is all I'm saying." She mumbled again, "You don't have to be. You may find it hard to believe, but I still love you because I know who you really are is somewhere in there. It may be buried a little deep, but you're still the brother who use to come get me with the flashlight when I called for you because I was scared to go to the bathroom at night in the dark." She stood and looked back tenderly at him before entering the house,

Inside the conversation had returned to the familiar words from the first night they had all arrived at the house.

"Momma, I know you don't want to hear it, and even if you don't want to move in with me, I think you should sell the house and maybe buy something small near me, especially with June talking about moving to Atlanta. I mean it could be good for you," Diane stated very matter-of-factly. Not soon after, the girls were all gone and Josephine was left in that big old house alone.

Josephine thought about what the girls had been saying ever since they had left, and she was beginning to think maybe they were right. She loved her church, and she would miss her grandchildren, but she needed a new beginning. She was young enough to start a new life since the first one hadn't worked out so good. Maybe her later days would be far greater than her former days. But change was scary, especially in one's sixties. Maybe that's really why she never left Jim. She loved him though and always hoped he would change, but she knew deep down it would never happen.

After the hell she had been through with Jim, she was content being alone. She never wanted to take that kind of risk again. Logically, she knew all men weren't like that. She had seen proof, but she was too afraid to chance it. She sat at the kitchen table, sipping a cup of coffee, asking God to guide her and help her make the right decision pertaining to not just the move, but life itself. She was at a crossroad, and she knew it. Did she believe the words in the Bible that she always wanted others to believe in and live by? She had faith for everyone else, but never quite enough for herself.

Josephine had found God long ago. She knew the Bible like she had written it herself, but there was a small piece of her that wondered why a God so great, so mighty, so powerful, so loving could have allowed her to endure all she had at the hands of Jim. She didn't blame Him, but she wondered why he didn't warn her not to get involved with him. Maybe he had, but she just didn't want to see the signs. She was so enamored with Jim when she met him. If God had ridden down on a cloud with a bolt of lightning in his hand and threw it between her and Jim and them stepped down from the cloud and said, "Josephine, Jim is not the one!" with a thunderous roar, she wouldn't have believed God himself.

Besides, she was pretty naïve back then. Jim knew exactly what to say and do. He wasn't smooth, he was sho 'nuff smooth. But that was no longer relevant. The bottom line was she had no one to blame but herself. She could have left. Mabel would have helped her, and she knew it, but she was too proud. Everything was always gonna be okay, let her tell it. She knew there were women who had it much worse, and that's one way she justified staying.

As she sat there, she thought she kind of owed it to Diane to do something for her. She had done so much for Josephine and the girls. She always tried her best to save them, and if Diane wanted her there, then she would go. She got up from the table and went over to the phone and called Diane.

"Hi, Momma. Is everything okay?"

"Diane child, yes. Everything is fine. I've decided to come."

"What do you mean come?"

"Well, you said you'd feel better if I move there, so I think that's what I am going to do. I'm going to sell the house and maybe buy a small little house. I don't need much, but I have to have a yard for my garden."

"Why don't you just move in with me?"

"Well, I was thinking you're already going to have June there, and I don't want to crowd you. Plus, I like having my own space. Maybe June could even move in with me for a spell while she's trying to figure it all out."

"Okay, let's do it. I'm so excited. Have you told the others? Oh my, have you told Jim Jr.?"

"You know, Diane, I've had that boy have just as much control over me as his daddy, always covering for his foolishness and making excuses because of his father, then making excuses because he didn't have his father and blaming myself for allowing Jim to corrupt that boy. I know I'll have to answer for that someday, but I'm not going to live the rest of what life I do have left under the watchful eye of another Holloway man. I don't care what Jim Jr. thinks."

Diane sat on the other end of the phone in shock, wondering who this woman was impersonating her mother and exactly what she had done with her. She was ecstatic though. She couldn't help herself.

She had been wanting Josephine to move there ever since she had decided Atlanta would be home. Josephine hadn't told any of the children as she had just decided that morning, but Diane quickly put things in motion. She couldn't wait to call Jim Jr. and let him know Josephine was putting the house on the market. It gave her great joy. She didn't want to hate her brother, but seeing as how he was the spawn of Satan, she had no choice. She hated all things evil, and he was definitely an arrogant evil butthole in her eyes.

He and Honey got along a little better, maybe because they were closer in age. Honey would sometimes take up for Jim Jr. and say she kind of understood some of his nonsense. She was the only one he would halfway listen to, and she was the only one who could half tolerate him and his B.S.

It wasn't long before the plans were in motion. Jim Jr. had reluctantly listed the house even though he dealt mainly in commercial real estate, but not before giving Josephine a hard time. Well, actually, he initially forbid her from selling the house. How funny, a son forbidding his mother to do something, but he tried. He showed up at the house telling her how she couldn't sell the house and there was no way he would allow it.

Allow it, Josephine thought and merely laughed at him. "Not only will you allow, you will do it, or I'll simply get another agent who will–what did you say again?–'allow.'" She chuckled again and said, "You know, Jim Jr., I've dealt with your foolish ways for too long, and it ends today. If you can't respect me as your mother, you're no longer welcome in my life, period."

Jim Jr. stood there looking at her. She had never truly stood up to him before, There was something different in her eyes. They were alive, and her voice was firm and fiery, and he knew she was serious. There was a small level of respect she gained from him in this very moment.

"Now I love you, Jim—you're the only son I have—and I love my grandbabies, but I'm not going to live the remaining years of my life just existing. I've decided to live. I dang well deserve it. I've been through hell and back, and when I got back, I never gave myself permission to live, so screw you if you can't be the son I need you to be. This relationship has been one-sided and selfish on your part for far too long. And another thing: The next time you put your hands on Charlene, I'm going to call the police on you myself. I want you to go get some help, or so help me God, I'll have her leave you and take everything you have, and I mean it. I'll do it too. You watched the things your father did to me and how it broke me. How dare you do it to someone else? How dare you? It doesn't make you a man."

Jim Jr. couldn't say anything. You can best believe he wanted to as he would have done so many times in the past, but not this day. He knew she meant every word, and for some reason, in addition to be extremely confused, he was slightly scared.

He began to think on the things Honey had shared with him that day on the front porch as he had done since the girls' departure. He didn't want to end up like Jim, but how could he not? How could he change? He had always looked up to his father and thought he was the greatest and the coolest. There were not many dads like him, especially Black ones. He was just different. In spite of what others saw as shortcomings, Jim Jr. worshipped the ground he walked on.

This was the father God had given them, and he knew he favored him over the girls, but he had no idea his father had attempted to molest Honey until she shared with him that day on the porch. He had no respect for women, and he learned that from Jim, but he knew he had a good wife, just like Josephine, but he was never taught to value those things about a woman, and he was now finally beginning to understand not only that it was wrong, but why it was wrong.

He never thought twice about the abuse his mother suffered, verbally or physically, at the hands of Jim. He was taught that was how you earned respect, strong armed. He operated like that in every aspect of his life and that was why he was so successful. Jim Jr. wanted and had that same success.

He recalled how it felt riding around town with his father in that Cadillac. It was a fine car, and everyone knew it, liked it and wanted it. His father threw money around like it was nothing. It was so impressive to a young, impressionable boy, and he wanted to be just like him. Women loved Jim, and he kept no secrets from Jim Jr.

"This here between you and me, you hear? Between a father and his son. You don't go off tellin' your sisters and definitely not ya momma."

After a while, that line was no longer necessary. Jim Jr. knew where his loyalty lay, and it was with Jim. He knew all about Jane and never said a word. He got that honest too. Jim Jr. had stepped out on Charlene on occasion but never carried on a serious affair like Jim had with Jane. He was even beginning to question his own infidelity.

After his confrontation with Josephine, he called Honey.

"Hey." She sounded puzzled. "Is everything okay?" she said, answering the phone, seeing it was a call from the brother who never called.

"*Ummm,* hey, yes. I mean no. I mean…"

"Is it Momma?" Honey got worried.

"No, nothing like that. I was just thinking, you know. I just finished talking to Jo, and *ummm,* she told me she is thinking about moving to Atlanta and wants to sell the house."

"*Ummm,* okay. Wow. I hadn't gotten the word yet, but okay. It's probably going to be good for her, you know?"

"Yes, I know. I've just been thinking about things since we talked that day, and I want to be different, Honey. I don't want my kids to hate me. I don't want Charlene to hate me. I don't know why I do some of the stuff I do. I just don't know any other way, and I don't want to look weak."

Honey was taken aback, but she was glad he called. She couldn't believe it was happening, but nonetheless, she was glad. She explained to him it would be hard and that change didn't come overnight, but if he was willing to put the work in, he could be different. He could be a better man than Jim ever was and definitely a better husband.

"You just gotta be real with yourself and what you want out of life. Who are you trying to impress, the people in the streets? What does that matter if you have no love and respect in your own house? Start by making things right with Charlene. It won't make you look weak, if anything, only a strong man can admit the way he has been doing things is wrong and take the steps to change it. Your marriage could be so much better. She loves you now. Can you imagine how much more she would love you if y'all were a team—if you respected her and didn't cheat on her, and for God's sake, stop putting your hands on her?"

He thought about how beautiful his wife was, and it made him think about how pretty Josephine was in earlier pictures and how her looks had slowly changed over the years but how she began to become pretty again after Jim died. He didn't really want that for Charlene. Deep inside, he loved her. He just didn't know how to express it in a healthy way. He always thought she was lucky to have him, but who knows, how far she would have gone in life because she was really smart, and sometimes that intimidated Jim Jr., the same as it had with Jim Sr. That was the real reason he wanted her home with the children. He was afraid that she might find somebody better or realize he wasn't as great as he appeared.

This child was all messed up, but he was willing to try, and that spoke volumes to Honey. She was on board with helping him with this transition. She knew her brother wasn't perfect, and she had always secretly prayed he would grow up and really become a man, and it looked as if her prayers were finally being answered. Now, she was conflicted. She didn't know if she should get a glass of champagne and celebrate or find the nearest open church and go thank God for his faithfulness. Maybe both!

It wasn't easy for Jim Jr. He had no idea where to start. He was still young enough to change but had dug such a hole of despair he didn't know how he would find his way out. Men have not always been the first to jump at going to counseling, especially Black men. They fought their own demons, confided in one another and never let on what they were really feeling. Manhood was synonymous with strength, and there was no way he could be perceived as weak. No way.

He thought about calling the church office to make an appointment to maybe talk things over with the pastor, but he couldn't bring himself to do it. He, like his father, had an image to uphold, and he didn't want anyone thinking less of him. He felt embarrassed and ashamed, two feelings he had never experienced in all his life of shenanigans. Where was this coming from and why now? He had the overwhelming sensation to call his wife and tell her he loved her, but he didn't.

Jim looked up at the ceiling. "God, if you're up there—I mean if you're really real—I need your help. I want to do better. I want to be better, but I don't know how to start. I don't know what to do. Help me!" he cried out. His eyes welled with tears, which he refused to let fall. He thought about how much he missed his father, but on the same hand, how betrayed he felt, knowing now what he'd tried to do to Honey. The inner turmoil was causing his heart to race and his palms to sweat. All of a sudden, there was an unexplainable peace that came over him, like a slow rush of warm water enveloping him from his chest and simultaneously spreading outward through his entire body, and he couldn't help but let those stubbornly held tears release.

That night after the kids were in bed, he waited for Charlene to get them settled, and as she entered the room, he just stared at her. She was nervous and didn't really know what to make of it.

"Are you alright, babe? Can I get you anything before I get in the shower?"

"No. I'm good." He motioned for her to come to him.

She sensed something different, but she was unsure and still slightly afraid. She didn't know if she had done something that may have upset him or what. He was acting awfully strange compared to what she was used to.

"I'm, *uhhh,* not really good at this, Charlene." He took her hand as she sat next to him on the chaise longue in their bedroom. "*Ummm,* I just, *uhhh,* need you to know I'm sorry, you know. I'm sorry for not being the kind of husband you thought I was going to be. You know I—" He searched for the words he needed in order to express the level of regret he felt, but there was nothing that could erase some of the things he had said and done to her. "I just want you to know I want to do things different, okay?" He looked over at her again. His knee shook nervously up and down. "I'm not saying I can be perfect or anything, but I can be better."

She sat there attempting to take it all in, wondering who this strange man was in Jim Jr's body. She saw a glimpse of the person he was before they had gotten married, the young man who swept her off her feet and sold her the dream of a wonderful life together, but she didn't quite know what to make of it. Was he dying? she thought. What was really going on in that brain of his? Had he gotten some other woman pregnant? Was this a cruel joke? All kinds of thoughts flooded her mind. But she was afraid to say what she really thought because of how he may react, so she just sat and listened.

"I know I've hurt you physically and emotionally, but I'm going to start working on that, and I promise I'll never lay my hands on you again. I just thought you know...well, that was my way of keeping you in line. I know it sounds crazy, but I really don't want to ever do that again, and I don't want to lose you. I need you, and I've never admitted to needing anyone in my life— ever. Nobody, man."

He jumped up, pacing, slightly agitated by the vulnerability he was putting on display, but deep down, he knew he could trust her with his feelings and it would never leave that room. She always had his back. Even when he was wrong, she was faithful to him in every way, even if it meant putting herself last.

The good thing was he did really love her, and they still had fun together when they weren't fighting, which wasn't all the time. She knew he had affairs, and she just dealt with it, which is how the fights initially began, and after a while, she just learned to live with it, so she was curious, especially since he claimed he was never going to put his hands on her again. This new and improved man, was he going to stop cheating on her? She drummed up enough nerve to ask.

"Can I ask you something?" She stared past him and into the closet.

"Anything."

"Don't get angry, please, but I need to know if you're going to stop cheating on me." She braced herself with the uncertainty of not knowing how he would respond to her. Would he yell, smack her because he felt disrespected or just walk out. Surprisingly, none of the above transpired.

He wasn't expecting that question, but he was more than willing to answer. "These women out here don't mean nothing to me. It's just something I do—I mean did. So yeah, I'm going to try to stop that too."

"You're going to try? Does somebody have a hold on you like that, that you can't just walk away?'

"No. It's not like that." He stumbled over his words. "I'm just trying to say I'm not about to be out there looking for anything, and I'm going to try and do my best to not get caught up in anything."

"Hmmm," she released from her tired lips.

"Give me a break, Charlene. This is new for me, okay, and I'm coming to you because I love you, and I want to have a real marriage—a better marriage. I want to be the kind of man my kids are proud of, you know?"

"You must forgive me. I just don't even know how I'm supposed to react right now. I'm in shock for one, and I just don't want to get my hopes up and then things don't change is all.

She wanted this to be real but wondered how and why. How would he change and why now? She had always loved him in his imperfect self. She remembered the side of him that wooed her and gave her the smile she'd worn so beautifully until he began to change, so why should she set herself up to be betrayed yet again? He would have to show and prove, not tell and prove, and in the meantime she would remain as she was, consistent and not too vulnerable. That way if the bottom fell out, it would be as if there had never been support there anyway.

As the weeks progressed, she noticed the change, but she was still not all in. She couldn't risk it, however, so far, she was enjoying the "changed man."

Jim Jr. felt frustrated at times because he wanted to be rewarded for his efforts, even if it was words of appreciation for his behavior change, but Charlene looked at it as if this was what he as a husband should have been doing all along. She wasn't giving out cookies and milk for things Jim should have been doing. Wanting to be rewarded for being faithful and not smacking your wife from time to time does not constitute a reward. What was wrong with some men? It truly baffled her and many like her.

Jim Jr. arrived home from work in time for dinner as he had been doing for several weeks. They sat at the table and ate as a family while laughing and talking about the day, but Jim Jr. noticed Charlene was still being a little reserved. He was changing, but she wasn't. She still wasn't letting him in, and it angered him. Couldn't she see how hard he was trying? Why was she making this so hard for him? She began to clear the dishes when he offered to help.

"Hey, let me do this while you get the kids bathed and ready for bed."

"Are you sure?" she responded, dazed and stunned. He never helped clean anything. She always waited on him hand and foot, and it wasn't that she minded initially when things were good between then, but after he began to change, she no longer felt he deserved it.

"Yes, baby, I'm positive. Let me know when you get ready to put them down, and I'll come in for story time."

Now this was all too much. She had to be living in some alternate universe. Aliens had surely inhabited his body and taken him to the mother ship.

"Uh, okay. Sure. That would be nice."

He cleared the table and cleaned the kitchen before heading upstairs to shower. As he got out the shower, there was a small knock at the door. "Story time, Daddy."

"Okay, give me one sec, and I'll be ready."

"Okay," the little voice squeaked.

He quickly toweled off, jumped into his pajamas and headed down the hall. It was great. He sat in the rocking chair with Charlene in his lap as she read the story. He listened to the sound of her voice, and he watched the intensity in his children's faces as they lived the story she read vicariously through their mother's voice, facial expressions and emotions. Even if it was a story she had read before, they sat there as if it were the first time hearing it. Jim Jr. realized what he had been missing out on, and his heart felt full. Tears filled his eyes, and this time, he couldn't stop them.

"Daddy, are you crying?" his five-year-old son asked.

"No, I'm not crying."

"Yes, you are," his daughter said.

"Men don't cry, Daddy," his son said.

"What's wrong, Daddy?" his daughter shoved her brother and asked.

He attempted to pull himself together. He cleared his throat and tried to suck it up, but the floodgates were open, and no matter how he tried to stop the water, there was no use.

"What's wrong, babe?' Charlene turned to him.

"*Ahhh,* I'm good. I'm good. Let me up." He left the room quickly.

"I'll be right back, kids. Vanessa, you can go on down to your room. I'll be back to tuck both of you in."

Charlene went to the bedroom to find Jim Jr. sitting next to the bed. She sat on the floor next to him but didn't say a word. He put his head in her lap and cried until there were no tears left, and not until the last tear fell was he able to finally speak.

"I love you so much." He sat up, holding her hands, looking her in her eyes. "I am so, so sorry for everything. You guys mean everything to me, and this is the life I want. I don't want to be out in the streets. I don't want the love and respect of anyone out there if I don't have it from you guys." He kissed her softly but passionately, and she felt the sincerity, and she believed every word he said. This was the beginning of something great for them and their family.

"I need to go tell Joseph something. I'll be right back."

"Okay. I'm going to go tuck Vanessa in," she said.

After she prayed with Vanessa and tucked her in, she stood in the doorway and listened to him try to undo some of the flawed thinking he had already begun to feed Joseph.

"Son, real men do cry. There's nothing wrong with crying, just not all the time." He laughed. "But sometimes if you have certain feelings inside or if you hurt yourself or something, it may make you want to cry, and that doesn't mean you're not a man, okay?"

"But you said boys who cry are punks."

"I did say that, and well, your daddy was wrong, okay? So, I'm trying to tell you the right way now."

Charlene came in while he said his prayers. They both kissed him goodnight and headed out the room. She put her hand in his, and for the first time in a long time, she had hope.

One Last Time

I t was definitely déjà vu. Just a few months prior, they were all back there thinking there was something wrong with their mother. Now, as they arrived back at the house one by one, it was a happier time. A much happier time. This was the final chapter in the saga of Jim. The house had been sold, and it was time to pack it up and move forward with life. The girls each came to get rid of things they had left or to pack up things they wanted to keep.

Diane was the first to arrive, As she pulled up, she stared at the outside of the house wondering if the windows would shed tears at the absence of the Holloways. She couldn't be more excited, yet the reality of failed to seem real. She didn't really believe Josephine was going to go completely through with it, but she had, and now she had three weeks to be out of the house. Josephine claimed she had been packing up things here and there, but when Diane arrived, she saw tons of cardboard boxes lined up against the wall still in bundles. Exactly what she had packed remained to be seen.

She decided to start in the kitchen because that would be the hardest. Josephine loved to cook, so she had so much stuff. None of the girls really enjoyed cooking that much. They were too busy trying to be liberated. They would cook, but not like their mother. Even when they got a microwave, Josephine refused to use it. She reheated food on the stove or in the oven, and she was still that way.

"I'm not putting my food in anything that shoots rays at it to cook it, reheat it or whatever else they are made for." She would spout that anytime anyone mentioned using the "death ray box" as she lovingly named it. She just believed it was not normal or healthy to nuke food as the term became widely known.

"No one has ever died from using a microwave," the girls would often say every time she said anything about them microwaving food. Her rebuttal was always the same: "That you know of." When they first got one, it was, "It hasn't been out long enough to know if it's safe." Even with no fast-breaking news stories of microwave deaths, she was stuck in her ways. Diane laughed as she thought of that, but that was her mother, and she wasn't going to change that. It's funny how a few weeks prior, there were nothing but bitter, tragic hidden memories, and now those memories seemed to be overshadowed by some of the good ones. Even after Jim had passed, they sometimes still walked around on eggshells as if there was some way he would come back and continue his reign over them.

Diane came across a small teacup she had made in home economics in like the third grade. It was tucked in the back with other prized possessions of Josephine's. She was so proud of that warped mug that she swore was a teacup, and finding it there reminded her how proud Josephine was too. It was amazing how much stuff she had kept from their childhood. The things that were invaluable were what she held near to her heart. She continued to pull, wrap and box until there were four cabinets completely empty with what seemed like a zillion more to go.

She wanted her sisters to be there with her carrying the packing load, but Honey and June both couldn't come until that

Friday. Diane really needed to be at work, but truthfully, she was trying to escape—escape everything that constituted her life at this point. To the onlooker, she had accomplished so much, but she was emotionally bankrupt. She didn't really realize how much of life had passed her by while she was out saving the world. Now she wondered what was next, or better yet, what was left. The awards and accolades? The feeling when she helped someone?

These were not trivial things nor was she ungrateful for them, but she was so empty at the end of the day when it was her and herself in her house that was supposed to be filled with baby cries, toddler laughter and little feet running from room to room. Where her husband would cuddle her at the end of a long day and rub her feet after she'd been in heels and a power suit all day. The family that would encourage her when she felt like she didn't measure up in a field where the good old boys club always trumped what was right and where being a woman, let alone a Black woman, was hard enough. She had experienced racism and sexism firsthand on many occasions, and it hardened her even more, and maybe that's why she was always able to put her feelings in a box and put a nice tidy bow on them whenever things didn't go her way.

This new feeling of emptiness was one she was not ready for, and she had no idea how to deal with it. She had never cried in her entire life as much as she had since coming home a few months prior.

Diane was an emotional wreck, and she had always hated emotions. They were the enemy. They let people in, and when they get in, they will exploit your weakness. This is what she had learned from a very young age, and she had lived by it and never forgotten it. So how could she reconcile these new emotions with her emotionless self? How could she long for Richard the way she did, and how could she begin to start having hopes and expectations now after being equipped for so long to not have them and being okay with it?

After several hours of packing, she had had enough and seemed to be getting nowhere. The boxes were filling and stacking, but why did it look as if no progress was being made? She went up and showered.

"Do you wanna go get something to eat, Momma?" She peeked into Josephine's room and found her sitting on the bed.

"No. I'm not too hungry, and there are a few things I want to take care of in here before I go to bed."

"Well, don't overdo it. I'm just going to run and grab a shoulder sandwich. Do you want anything?"

"No. I'm going to have some fruit."

"Alright, suit yourself. Love you."

"Love you too. Thanks for coming to help your old mom."

"Oh, please. I keep telling you, you're not old, and when you get to Atlanta, you're going to see. It's time for you to live, lady. *Whoo hoo.* It's time."

June and Honey arrived as scheduled Friday afternoon but were too tired do anything other than eat and talk.

"I'm going to let y'all slide tonight, but tomorrow, we have to get busy. I mean we got a lot done, but there's still so much left." Diane eyeballed them.

Honey stood from the chair in the living room and headed into the dining room. She opened the buffet drawer to begin going through it in order to divide and conquer the keeps from the throwaways.

"Wow, I can't believe she has pictures of Jim in here."

"You're kidding, right?" Diane looked irritated.

"Uh, no." Honey tossed the framed pictures on the dining room table.

"Toss that crap in the trash."

Josephine was walking in from the kitchen.

"Toss what in the trash? Don't be in here devaluing my valuables," she said jokingly.

"That trash." She pointed to the pictures of Jim, which also included a picture with him and Josephine.

"Don't you dare."

"You can't be serious. You can't want to keep pictures of that man."

"That man is your father, and he's dead. Don't disrespect the dead."

"No, he was your husband. I don't have a father." Diane was aggressive in her tone, almost combative, and she never spoke to Josephine in that way. There was something about Jim that could set her off to the point of no return.

"You know, Diane, you're so angry. Jim was my husband, and though he's gone, he gave me the best part of himself, and that's all of you. Without him, there would be no you."

"Yeah, well, maybe that would have been for the better. It would have saved me a whole lot of pain and heartache."

"I'll be the first to admit Jim had his flaws."

Diane cut her off. "Flaws? Flaws? Is that what they were, flaws? Picking your teeth is a flaw, showing up late to work is a flaw. Beating your wife half crazy is not a flaw, Mother. What is wrong with you?"

"I don't have to stand here and justify myself to you, Diane. You don't always know everything, and some things you don't need to know. At one time, your father was a very different man, but sometimes life has a way of taking even some of the best men and turnin' 'em bad, and that was the case with Jim. That's all water under the bridge. I honored my husband like the Bible said and did all I knew to do as a good wife. God saw Jim wasn't going to change, and he made a way of escape for me. He saved me from Jim's wrath, which was only getting more and more severe."

"Oh my God, you're killing me, always giving God credit for everything. God didn't save you from Jim. I did... It was me. I saved you."

The tears burst from her eyes like a volcano erupting. Her voice cracked as her sob-covered words continued. "And I wasn't just trying to save you. I was looking out for all of us, which was something you didn't have the courage to do. Jim was the devil, Momma. She could hardly contain herself. She began to shake. "He was the devil," she screamed loudly and violently. Her body continued to tremble, and her vision blurred.

A heavy, hovering silence took a seat in the room as June stood, and Honey allowed the wall to support. Time was held captive by her words. The moment was frozen. No one spoke or moved, What could be done or said to reverse the time and put Diane's words back in her mouth? Nothing could be done. The letters were out there now strung together dancing on air exposing new secrets. Josephine suffered from the same frozen state as the girls.

"I said it, okay? There it is. I said it." Diane broke the prolonged silence.

"Shut your mouth, Diane. Shut your mouth. Do you understand me?" Josephine looked as stern as she ever had, her eyes were wide and her heart raced to nowhere, but Diane couldn't stop the words from flowing. She was releasing the heaviest burden she had ever carried. "If you don't close your mouth—" Josephine gritted her teeth—"I will close it for you."

"Well, it's true."

"I said that's enough, Diane," Josephine yelled, which was out of character for her.

But it wasn't enough in Diane's eyes. With every word, she was rolling that boulder off her chest. She was breathing uninhibited. "Just like the last time I tried to tell you and you wouldn't listen. You didn't want to know, but maybe you have always known. Maybe you suspected, and like everything else, you refused to deal with it." Diane had never spoken to Josephine in this way.

Honey stood there confused. "What are you saying, Diane?"

"Alright, Diane, I think you better calm down and just think about what you're saying. Just stop already. Please." June stood, stepping in front of her pleading with her.

"Oh no, I'm just getting started. Where was God when Jim raped me in the middle of that floor?" She pointed into the living room. "Where was he, huh? I want to know where God was and how he could create something so evil and you stand here talking about flaws. Oh boy, that's some flaw."

"What?" Josephine's eyes followed Diane's pointed finger to the living room. "He did what?" Her voice was almost unrecognizable due to the shock of what she'd just heard. She was confused, and her brain seemed to shut down.

June began to weep silently. Honey put her arms around her. "It's okay, Junebug."

"I'm sorry, June. I just, I just… I just couldn't hold it in anymore, you know? I'm tired. I am sooo tired, June."

"No, it's not that." She looked up at Diane. "I thought it was just me." She leaned onto Honey, barely holding herself up. "I thought it was just me. I didn't want to tell anyone because I was so ashamed, and that night Jim was after Honey and she came in my room, I thought he was gonna do to her what he had been doing to me."

"Oh my Lord. What are you all saying?" Josephine grabbed her head and began to back up, not knowing where she was backing. Everything was numbingly loud, yet deafeningly silent. Time stood still, and she was no longer there. She was fading out of the scene as if she was having an out-of-body experience. She seemed disoriented. She began spinning and groping at the air, attempting to find something to help her balance herself, and though she felt the wall, it didn't hold her. She fell backward as she passed out, hitting her head on the dining table as she went down.

"Momma," Honey screamed.

"Call 911," Diane screamed.

"This is your fault," Honey screamed. "You just had to keep going, didn't you? You're not in court, and Momma isn't on trial. See what you did?"

"Why are you mad at me?' Diane shouted.

"That's enough," June screamed as she grabbed the phone to call 911.

Diane ran upstairs and grabbed her purse and keys and headed for the front door.

"Where are you going?" Honey shouted.

"It's better if I'm not here." Diane looked back, rolled her eyes and slammed the door.

Honey and June were too worried about Josephine to deal with Diane at that point. They waited frantically for the ambulance to arrive. Honey kneeled at Josephine's side while June paced from the door to Honey and back to the door. Honey noticed blood coming from the back of Josephine's head as she attempted to raise it and place it in her lap. Josephine was still unconscious. She had hit her head pretty hard. The sirens were heard in the distance, and a bit of relief was felt by them both. The fire department arrived first and asked a bunch of questions.

June left out the part about their father raping them, which was the root cause of their mother blacking out and hitting her head on the table. She simply said they were all talking and she seemed to look a little dizzy, and the next thing you know, she was falling. The paramedics arrived shortly thereafter and were briefed by the fire department on Josephine's condition and vitals before transporting her to the hospital.

"Did one of you want to ride over with her?"

"Maybe you should, in case she wakes up," June said to Honey.

"No, we'll just follow you."

"No, Honey, go with Momma. I'll be fine."

"I said no. Come on. Let's go."

So they did. They jumped in Josephine's car and headed over to the hospital. Honey finally broke the deafening silence, her expression was of pity mixed with love and a little admiration. She couldn't believe Jim had molested June and that she never said anything, and it made her wonder if Josephine knew. She reasoned she couldn't have known and stayed, and that's where she was going to remain in order to keep her own sanity. This was getting crazier by the visit. Honey was just ready to leave it all behind and get back to her life in New York with Jared. She didn't care if she ever set foot in Ohio ever again. She was looking over at June wondering if it was okay to ask her about it.

"Stop staring at me!" June felt Honey's eyes talking to her.

"Don't holler at me. I just…well, I was just wondering if you were okay. I mean you said 'what he had been doing' like it was more than once."

"It's over. That was so long ago, and I really just want to leave the past where it belongs, in the past."

"Did you go see somebody about it?"

"No. I said I don't want to talk about it. I didn't then and I don't now okay, Honey? I'm not trying to be mean. I just want to forget it happened. I hate I even brought it up. I don't want pity, and I don't want people looking at me like I'm damaged goods. It's not like I wanted it to happen but sometimes I knew if I didn't, he would do something to Momma."

Honey sat in the seat, antsy, wanting to ask more questions but not wanting to upset June. She couldn't even imagine what that must have been like. This was the first time Honey actually said aloud she was glad Jim was dead. She knew he was mean and ornery and used to beat their mother, but that never caused her to revel in his death. She was never quite as angry as June and Diane, and now she understood their rage toward him—their unsympathetic viewpoint that never seemed to waiver. She completely and totally understood, and she looked over at June and said "I'm glad he's gone." She couldn't quite muster up enough hate to say *dead,* but gone was close enough. Her eyes glazed over as she stared past June out the window.

"Thanks, Honey. I really am okay. I don't even think about it anymore. It's just when Diane said that, it brought it back."

Arriving at the hospital, Honey jumped out and went in with the paramedics and Josephine while June parked the car. Josephine was now awake but laying there and was told not to try and speak.

"Momma, it's Honey."

"Honey, okay, listen we're going to take her in the back, and I'll be out as soon as the doctor says you can come back, okay?" The paramedic pointed to the waiting area. "The front desk is going to call you over to get more information."

"Why can't I come with her?"

"They are probably going to get a CT scan, then they'll know more. Don't worry. I'll make sure to tell them to come for you as soon as the doctor says it's okay."

"We'll take good care of her," the nurse said as she opened the doors to receive Josephine.

The paramedics continued to call out information about Josephine to the nurse as they all went through the double doors. Honey felt helpless as she stood watching the gurney disappear down the hall as the doors closed slowly behind them.

Just then June came in, and Honey was tearful as Josephine was taken. She explained what the nurse had said, and they waited and waited and waited for what seemed like an eternity.

A Glass of Wine

D iane just drove around. She wanted to call Richard because he was really the only person she ever felt really close to besides her sisters. She knew she needed him but that he couldn't be there for her after how she had ended things and his coldness when she tried to reach out to him a few months prior. Life was not supposed to be this hard, and she wondered who she could speak with to get a do-over. She wanted to blame Jim or Josephine or anybody, but she knew to find the true culprit in the demise of her relationship, she only had to look into any object that would reflect her image. She wanted to be a different person, but she didn't know how, and it was probably too late to start.

Besides, it wouldn't bring Richard back, and she couldn't imagine loving anyone but him if she was being completely honest with herself, which seemed to be the common theme in these visits home. It's like they brought up something in her, good and bad. Some days her emotions were light enough to ride the wings of a butterfly while other days they were the matador in a bullfight. They were uncontrollably, and she hated that.

She found herself pulling up at a restaurant because she wanted—no needed, she told herself—a drink and some food. How could she be thinking about food when she didn't even know what was going on with her own mother, but she was angry with Josephine. And until that day, she never realized it and to the extent the masked anger had grown until it emerged. The level of anger she felt was previously unimaginable. In her mind, she began to ask some of the same questions Honey had asked: Did Josephine know?

Diane reasoned that it was the one time, and he definitely wouldn't have told on himself, but now with June saying what she said and making it seem like it happened more than once, it made her wonder. But she didn't know, and she and June were pretty close, so she came to the same conclusion as Honey: She didn't know. There was no way she would have stayed with him if she knew, but why was she so oblivious? Why didn't she know? *We were her children. Why didn't she save us?*

She sat in the car and began to cry yet again. Who was this weak woman she was becoming? This emotional basket case that could not compose herself. The ocean waves of thoughts crashed down upon her mind, flooding her logic. There was no way she would have stayed if she knew, and why didn't God tell her since they talked so much? The thoughts made her angry all over again—at Josephine but most of all at God.

After pulling herself together once more, she went in and was seated without delay. A glass of wine was ordered almost immediately, followed by a medium-rare steak, loaded baked potato and a house salad. She was ready for her second glass before the food arrived.

"I am not trying to be nosey," the waiter said.

"Then don't be," she responded, not looking up from the magazine she had taken from her purse and began thumbing through while waiting. "*Ummm,* okay then." He turned to walk away.

"Wait. Brandon, right?" He nodded in affirmation. "Okay, Brandon. I'm really not a mean person, but I seem to be having a mental breakdown over here, so I really just want to be left alone so I can drink my wine, read about articles that clearly do not apply to my joke of a love life and eat my steak. Are we good?" She glanced up.

"Yes. I just wanted to make sure you were okay and see if you needed anything because you look stressed out like you've been crying is all. You might actually want to put your sunglasses back on to cover your puffy eyes so concerned citizens won't stop and check on you."

"Brandon, little sweet Brandon. How old are you, twenty-five?"

"I'm twenty-eight, actually," he said proudly.

"Okay, Brandon who is twenty-eight and clearly proud of it. I don't mean to be funny, but there's nothing you have gone through in your little twenty-eight years on earth that could have equipped you to be in the position to help me, but I'll have to say, I appreciate your thoughtfulness."

"Try me." He smiled.

"What?" She turned toward him, puzzled.

"I said try me. My shift ends in—" he looked down at his watch— "forty-three minutes. Can I invite myself to come back to talk with you?"

"Why?"

"Because you look heavy. Life is weighing you down, so this is what we're going to do: I'm going to let you finish eating, reading

your little magazine and drinking your wine. When you're done, I am
going to take you somewhere quiet, let you unload and get it all out,
then we're going to go have some fun—bowling, movies, live music,
whatever you want. The only stipulation is you have to enjoy
yourself, no tears after you unload because you look as if you should
be cried out right about now. Alright I'll be back with your food
shortly." He smiled the most beautiful warm, confident smile you
could have imagined.

Diane sat there and actually for a moment pondered if this was
for real. Why would she tell this child anything about her life? When
he came back with her food, he smiled that perfect straight-teeth
smile, and she wondered if he was actually flirting with her or if he
was really just trying to be nice. It wasn't like she was old, just older
than him, and it's not like she wasn't pretty. Who was she kidding?
She had passed pretty years ago. She was dangerously sexy. They all
were, all three Holloway girls, and she definitely kept in shape, but
she was being silly. What could this man-child want with her?

She was seriously entertaining it, but in her heart of hearts,
she knew she needed to go check on Josephine. After all, she had no
idea what was going on with her. She took her phone out to call
Honey, but immediately slid it back into her bag. She didn't know
what to feel. She was still angry, but she had calmed down and was
now a blanket of shame covered her along with the embarrassment of
her behavior. How could she disrespect Josephine like that? How
could she deliberately hurt her? She had to know it couldn't end well,

but once she got started, she just couldn't hold back. The box was opened, and there were no amount of nails that could hold the top on.

After her third glass of wine, Brandon confidently strolled over asking if she was ready.

"I'm scared if I leave you here much longer you are going to need another bottle of wine." He laughed though he was very serious.

"Well, I still need my check, and I actually did want some dessert." She didn't really want dessert. However she did want control.

"Alright, well let's hit it. I already took care of your check, and as for dessert, we can go anywhere you want for dessert, just not here because this is where I work, and I'm so ready to be off."

Before she knew it, she had allowed him to guide her from the booth and gave no resistance whatsoever. They walked to his car, which was nicer than she anticipated it to be. She wasn't afraid of going somewhere with this man she didn't even know. Something in her told her it was alright. Besides, if something were to happen to her, the evidence would lead straight to him. Her car was still parked there. They were seen talking and hopefully leaving together. Yep, he would be going away for a long time, she thought. He opened the door, and she slid in. She watched him as he glided around the front of the car. He was sexy. There was no denying that. This beautiful, beautiful specimen was something to behold.

They talked a little as he drove, to where she didn't know. She leaned her seat back as they made small talk. She listened but watched the buildings whiz by as they drove.

"Okay, so what type of dessert are you thinking because I'm thinking cheesecake or apple pie maybe?"

"I'm thinking a big ice cream sundae, but if you know where we can get some good cheesecake, I'll take it." The weight continued to lift from her.

"I got you." He looked over and smiled. Before long, they pulled up to a huge house in the small city of Shaker and stopped.

"Where are we?" she questioned.

"The only place I know that makes the best cheesecake, my mother's."

"Boy, I'm not going in here meeting your mother. It's bad enough I'm riding through the streets with a random stranger who is probably going to take me in here and chop me up or something or lock me in a box and make me a sex slave. *Ummm,* just take me back to my car, please? Seriously."

He could tell she was very serious, but he laughed. "Girl, stop playing. Ain't nobody trying to chop you up or make you a sex slave. What's wrong with you? Man, you pretty dark. I definitely need to bring some fun to your life." He walked around still chuckling and opened her door. "Come on. Whew, you funny."

She got out of the car a bit reluctantly. They walked up, and he rang the doorbell. "Oh, so you don't live with your parents?"

"No. Why?"

"I was just wondering since you're ringing the doorbell and not just going in."

"Yeah, no. I don't just walk in my parents' house unless they are expecting me. I respect their privacy. Besides, one of the things my dad always said was that when I moved he was walking around naked every chance he got, so yeah, I always ring the bell."

They both laughed.

"Well how do you know she has some cheesecake?"

"Because when I talked to her yesterday, she said she was making a cheesecake, and I told her I was going to come by sometime this weekend and get some. You sure are full of questions."

Just then the door opened. A beautiful, polished woman opened the door with perfectly arched eyebrows and the same gleaming white smile.

"Hi, Mom."

"Sweetie," she said while looking at Diane from the corner of her eye as if sizing her up.

After breaking their embrace, he went to introduce Diane, and at that very moment they both realized he never asked her name and she never volunteered it. Diane stuck her hand out. "Hi. I'm Diane." His mother shook her hand cordially but not very inviting.

"Diane was at the restaurant eating, and I told her I knew the best place in the world to get cheesecake and talked her into coming with me, and here we are. May we please have cheesecake?" He laughed.

The house was magnificently huge and beautifully decorated. They made their way to the kitchen following Patricia, Brandon's mother. "Have a seat." She motioned to the kitchen's vastly huge island, and they complied. Patricia asked Diane where she lived and what exactly she did for a living as she took the plates down, cut the cake and served it.

"I actually live in Atlanta. I'm here helping my mother. She just sold her house and is getting ready to move down South to be closer to my sister and me. My sister recently left California and moved to Atlanta as well."

"Oh, I didn't know you lived in Atlanta. How do you like it?" Brandon asked.

Patricia's brows raised, as if they could even go any higher. "You didn't know she lived in Atlanta?" She looked puzzled.

"Yes. We just met at the restaurant."

"Wait. I'm sorry, what?" she said.

"Yes. I could tell she needed something, someone. She wasn't herself, I could tell."

"How could you know she wasn't herself if you just met her?"

"I just knew."

"Look, I'm sorry for intruding. You have a lovely home, and it was very nice to meet you. Well, actually, it may have been nice to meet you under other circumstances. Right now, it just feels a little weird. Understandably so." She turned to Brandon. "I think it's best if you take me back to my car, please."

"No, you don't have to go," Patricia said, slightly letting her guard down.

"It's quite alright." Diane stood, waiting for Brandon.

"Okay, well let me get our cheesecake to go." He threw a big grin at Patricia.

"No, I'm good, but thank you." Diane seemed embarrassed.

"Well, I'm taking mine," Brandon said. "Trust me, if you taste it, you won't leave it." Diane cut her eyes at him. "Seriously, you won't." He laughed.

"Diane, really it's fine. You're welcome to stay and have some cheesecake." Patricia was very sincere in her offer, but Diane's mind was already made up, and once that was done, there was usually no turning back.

"I appreciate the offer, but Brandon was right. It's been a long and a bit of a traumatic day, and I'm truly not myself. In real life, I would never go off with a total stranger, but I needed to escape my life for a few hours, and here I am."

Tears filled her eyes. She felt herself fidgeting, and she thought, *Here we go again with these emotions.*

"Oh, honey." Patricia walked toward her and attempted to comfort her, but Diane pulled away.

"I apologize. I'm fine. Really, I am. Thank you for your hospitality." She headed toward the door. Brandon headed after her, but not before grabbing the cheesecake he had put in a Tupperware bowl.

Patricia grabbed his arm. "Why are you always trying to save someone? She's too broken and too old for you, Brandon."

"I love you, Mom. You were broken once too, remember?" And he headed for the door. "I'm not trying to date her. She needs something, and I think I can help her find what she needs. That doesn't mean it's me." He kissed her cheek.

Patricia watched as he walked out the door, and she knew he was right. She, too, was broken at one time, and she would never want him to be in a relationship with a woman who was anywhere near as broken as she was at one time. She wasn't judging Diane, but she and her husband had worked too hard parenting and praying for him not to find a woman who was whole—not perfect, but whole.

Diane was already in the car when he got out the door. He stooped down at the door, giving her cheesecake and a fork through the window. "You know you want it. Don't be stubborn." She snatched the fork from his hand and rolled her eyes. "I'm going to stay here until you try it. It'll make you feel better. I promise."

She removed the lid from the container, eased her fork into it and took a bite. "Oh my God. This is so good." It was like heaven, if there was a heaven. If there was, this was where this cheesecake was made. She closed her eyes and took another bite.

"Told ya." He smirked. Returning to the driver's seat, he took a small bite of his cheesecake. "So where to now? I was thinking we could go to the lake or park and just talk. I don't want to take you back to my place because I don't want you thinking I'm going to chop you up or put you in a box to be a sex slave and all." He nervously chuckled. "You must watch a lot of crime stories."

"Actually, I'm an attorney, so I see and hear a lot of things that stay with me and sometimes make me a little jaded. You're just a baby. I don't know if you have experienced anything in your life that just makes you different, that changes the way you think, the way you live, just you period." She was beginning to get frustrated, not with him, just frustrated at the way her life was turning out.

Diane actually didn't think it would be so bad going to his place, but she knew she needed to go to the hospital. She went on to explain to Brandon the day she was having without all the unnecessary background. He completely agreed she needed to be with her family, but for some reason, even though he didn't know her, he wasn't quite ready to let go.

"Let me take you."

"What?" She turned and looked at him.

"Let me take you—you know, to the hospital."

"You know this makes absolutely no sense, right?"

"Yeah." He smiled. "I know."

But yet they drove on.

"Who are you?" Her eyes pierced him.

"What you need right now."

"Ha. How would you know anything about what I do or don't need?"

"I just have a feeling you need me. I think I've been correct so far, wouldn't you say?" He looked over at her continuing his swin in confidence.

"*Ummm,* I'm not going to have sex with you if that's where you're going with all this."

"What? Why would you think that's even what I'm thinking?"

"So you mean to tell you that hasn't crossed your mind?"

"Okay, that's a hard question to answer. I'm being set up." He laughed and smiled that straight white-teeth smile yet again.

"How's that a setup?" Diane wondered what his story was. She really hadn't thought about it until now that maybe it was her who hoped secretly that is where it was headed. It had been a while, and though she knew it could go nowhere—nowhere at all—she examined him and thought what could it hurt.

"Well," Brandon began, "if I say I wasn't even thinking of sex then you might say why, am I not attractive enough or young enough or what's wrong with me?"

Diane smirked.

"And if I say how could it not have crossed my mind as attractive as you are, only a blind man could not see the possibility? Then you would think that's what I'm trying to do."

Diane burst out laughing, cutting him off. "Okay, so clearly you do want to have sex with me." She laughed even harder. "You're not old enough to ride this ride anyway."

"Man, whatever. Let's just go check on your mom."

After they arrived at the hospital, Diane went to the information desk to find out exactly where Josephine was. A few hours had passed, but she was still in the emergency room. Brandon remained in the waiting room of the ER while Diane went back only to receive the cold shoulder from both June and surprisingly Honey too.

"So what did the doctor say?" Diane asked.

"Oh, because you care now?" June blurted out.

"Damn, June, not now okay?" Diane's voice expressed the exhaustion of situation.

"This is all your fault. You just couldn't let it go."

"Yep. We got the newsflash, June. This is all my fault. I put my mother in the hospital. Okay. Okay. We got the newsflash. Are you happy now? Is that what you wanted me to say? Do you feel better now?"

Honey walked over and hugged Diane as Diane pulled away. "I'm okay, Honey. Really, it's fine."

"Girls, that's enough," Josephine whispered.

They stopped and looked over at Josephine. What was there to be said right now? There was no reset button in life. Were they just to brush this under the rug as they had done with so many other of life's tragedies?

"Momma, *ummm,* I apologize for my behavior. I just came to see how you were. I'm sorry." Diane leaned over and kissed Josephine's cheek. "I was so angry, and I took that out on you, and I shouldn't have done that. I didn't mean to disrespect you like that or raise my voice at you."

Josephine was weak but nodded and placed her hand on top of Diane's.

"I'm going to talk to the nurse since your daughter doesn't want to tell me what's going on, and I'll come see you tomorrow. Is that okay?"

"This is rich. It took you forever to come, and now you can't even stay when this is all your fault."

"Shhh." Josephine looked over at June.

"What do you want me to say, June? What do you want me to do to make you feel better because obviously this is about you and not momma?"

"Just go, Diane." June sighed.

"I don't need this. What's happening to us?" She turned and walked out.

"June, look what you did," Honey said hopelessly.

"Look what I did. This is her fault, trying to play God."

Honey went out after Diane and waited for her to finish talking to the nurse. They were going to admit Josephine. They had stitched the gash in her head, and she had a slight concussion that they wanted to observe. In addition, they wanted to keep her connected to the heart monitor. Even though she hadn't had a heart attack, they believed her passing out was an anxiety-induced heart murmur. Maybe she was getting anxious about the move, or maybe it was what Diane had said to her, but either way, Diane was tired—tired of holding on to the thing that had secretly been the thorn piercing her side her entire life. It was as if she could never move past a certain stage emotionally. People could look at her life and see her success for what it was, however, she was never quite able to see what all others saw. She could only see the failures—failed family, violated body, failed marriage, and most of all, the failure to conceive and carry a baby of her very own.

"Honey, I don't really want to talk, okay?"

"No, Dee, it's not okay. What's going on with you and all that stuff at the house about saving Momma or saving us? I mean where's all this coming from? What did you mean?"

"Oh, Honey, just stop. Stop it! You're not as naïve as you try to play. I'm sure you all know I was responsible for it all, for the taking the enemy out. Don't act like you weren't happy when Jim never came home—when you never had to fear what could or would happen next. Please don't act like it wasn't the best thing for us all."

"I'm not saying that it wasn't better when he was killed. I know I shouldn't say it because I'm not happy about it. I would have preferred if he just left us alone and went far, far away, but either way, it was better," Honey admitted.

"Yes, but if he had left and went away, we would always be wondering and scared this could be the day he returns. Besides, he wasn't ever going to go anywhere, and we both know that."

"But Diane, I'm saying, did you do it? Did you really…you know?" Honey whispered.

"Did I what? Make our lives better? Yes, Honey, I did, and I would do it again in a heartbeat."

Honey looked at her. She was speechless. This day was swallowing Honey up as it continued. She stood there dazed and overwhelmed with each passing minute. Her sister was a murderer and a lawyer. She wondered how Diane reconciled the two.

Diane felt Honey's judgment, and she couldn't take it. She had done everything she could to keep her safe. That night all started because Jim had come after her, and now she stood there with those eyes burning through her.

"Anyway, I'm just gonna go." Diane broke the stare. "The nurse just told me they're keeping Momma, and when she wakes up again, just tell her I'm sorry. I don't know what came over me, and I still don't know what I'm doing or feeling, but I have to breathe." She leaned back against the wall and took a deep breath. Tears filled her eyes, and she tried not to blink for fear they would escape and flood her cheeks.

"I never breathe, Honey. I've been holding my breath my whole life, and I realized today I need to breathe. It may sound selfish, and it may not be the perfect time, but I need to do this before I suffocate, you know?" Her eyes pleaded with Honey for understanding, and somehow Honey mustered up an approving look because in a way she did understand. She had felt trapped by life sometimes, and she had taken opportunities to breathe, so all she could do was hug her, nod and give her a gentle, reassuring kiss on the cheek.

"It's going to be alright if you just let it be, Diane. I love you, and we're here for you when you need us to be. June is mad, but you know she's here for you."

A half-hearted thanks escaped from her mouth as she turned and headed for the lobby. As she walked through the doors, Brandon was sitting there patiently waiting. He looked up when he saw her and stood.

"How's your mom?"

"She has a minor concussion, and she had to get stitches in the back where she hit her head on the table, but she's going to be okay. They're going to keep her though."

"How are you feeling?"

"Hell, I don't know, Brandon. I don't know much of anything at this very moment. I don't even know how I ended up here on probably one of the most vulnerable days of my life with a random stranger I hardly know sharing a very intimate part of my life. None of it makes any sense." She sunk down in the seat next to where he had been seated.

He took her by the hand and just sat there with her, neither of them saying a word, but she felt comforted, and maybe that's all she needed.

"Can I get you anything?" he asked.

"Uh, no." She hesitated. "Nope, I think I'm good." She leaned over and rested her head on his shoulder. "Thanks for being in the right place at the right time."

"You're most welcome."

"You know, if you need to leave, you can, I can always have my sister take me to pick my car up."

"No, I took you from your car, and I'll return you when the time is right, and that's not going to be anytime soon."

"I think I'm ready to head home anyway. I just don't want to go home, but I do want to stretch out and relax. Is it okay if I come to your house? I just don't want to be at my mother's house right now, and it's either that or get a hotel, and I guess that doesn't make much sense because I don't want to be alone. I said it. I really don't want to be alone. Is that alright to say?"

"You are just trying to come over." He laughed. "You ain't slick. I see you." He could tell she wasn't used to being vulnerable, and he wanted to break some of the heaviness by joking.

"Boy, please. It's not like that. You can just take me to my car." She sat straight up.

"Man, you're so serious and defensive. I was just joking with you. Why are you so tense and mad, girl? It's gotta be hard living life like that."

"Like what?" She stood, grabbing her purse.

"Like this, like how you are right now, just mad. Like I don't really know you or what happened today, so maybe you're not like this all the time, but if you are, you've gotta rethink some stuff is all I'm saying. Life is short, way too short to not balance the crazy with a whole bunch of happy, I'm just saying. You're too beautiful to be so angry."

"So if I was ugly, I could be angry?"

"Well, at least you may have a reason to be angry, because you're ugly."

They both laughed.

"Are you serious? I really hope you did not mean that. That was not nice. Funny, but not nice," She laughed again.

"I didn't, but I kind of did." He laughed even more.

Just then June came through the doors. As she walked passed, she did a double take when she saw Diane, then she realized she was with someone, and now she had no choice but to go over and see who this mystery man was that she felt close enough to bring to a family crisis. This was totally uncharacteristic of Diane.

When she looked up and saw June, she wished she had already left. She began to beat herself up mentally as to why she was dumb enough to sit in the hospital lobby with this friendly stranger. *Why? Why? Why?* she asked herself, but the damage was done, and she had no valuable answer to sooth her inner self, so she would have to meet June head-on in this very moment. She thought all her years in court would prepare her for things like this, but none of that mattered when it came to dealing with her family.

"*Ummm.* What is this?" June looked and pointed back and forth between Diane and Brandon.

"What do you mean?" Diane tried to play dumb.

Just then, Brandon stood and stuck his hand out and introduced himself. June reluctantly gave him a limp shake.

"I didn't ask who you were, I asked what this was. As in why are you here? I mean I don't know you, and Diane has never mentioned you, so while my mother is laying in a hospital bed basically because of you—" she looked over at Diane— "you're out here with this five-year-old doing what? I'm just trying to figure that part out."

Diane stood slowly with no response to June, looked over at Brandon and motioned for him to come on. She was ready to go. She wasn't going to stand there and allow June to berate her—no way, no how.

"Don't walk away, Diane." But walk away is exactly what she continued to do. "I guess that's your new thing, huh? Walking away. What's the matter, you can't deal with real life anymore? So used to everything having to play out in court."

"Screw you, June. Everything I did, I did for all of us, just remember that after you come down from blame mountain. You were always the oldest, but you did nothing to protect us. Now you want to throw your weight around. Well, the job is all yours. I'm done."

She and Brandon began to walk away again. Brandon turned and blurted, "Nice meeting you. I'm sorry it was not under better circumstances." He turned back to catch Diane's evil eye upon him. "Sorry. I have manners. I can't help myself. I was raised right. Blame my mother."

June watched the automatic doors shut behind them before continuing to the vending machine for more coffee.

"Wow! I don't even know who I am today. I don't know this woman who's not making every attempt to make it right and save the day. I'm not familiar with her altogether. This is sheer madness," Diane screamed at the top of her lungs. "I'm free. I'm free. For the first time in my life, I feel freeeeeeee." She threw her arms up in the air and spun around.

"*Ummm,* let's not do that again while on hospital grounds. They may really think you're mad and lock you up in the mental ward." He glanced over at the stranger who he seemed to know intimately, wondering how he ended up there and why. Was there a purpose to fulfill in this woman's life? He believed in purpose and destiny, and right now he knew he was destined to take this ride.

"I'm feelin' you, okay? I need you to know that. I think you need me for something for how long I don't know, but I'm down, okay? He looked over at her. "I need you to know that."

"*Hmmm.* Is that right?"

"Yeah, it's real. Believe that."

"Can you just take me to get my car? I mean I appreciate whatever this was today, but I just need to collect myself."

"You still wanna hang at my house?"

"No, I'm good. I'd probably better just get a hotel. I mean again, I don't really know you. I just keep forgetting that."

"You want me to come with you? He looked over, waiting for a response, but she said nothing. "I'm just saying, if you don't feel safe coming to my house but you just don't want to be alone, I don't mind coming to stay with you, if you need me."

"If I need you? What makes you think I need you? I'm tired of you trying to think you know me or could possibly know what I need."

"There you go again. That. That right there is how I know you need something, and right now, I'm what's available to you, and honestly what else do you have? A fight with your sisters? An empty hotel room? Come stay with me. You can sleep in my extra room."

"Just take me to my car." She leaned her head back as she thought about life and what the purpose was. What was the point of it all really? Why did she meet this young man? Maybe he was right.

Maybe she needed him but didn't want to admit it. She was always so busy caring for everyone else since she and Richard split. She pushed her feelings more and more to the side, not even wanting to hope for anything good. If she lived her life that way, she would never have to worry about disappointment or anything else that came along with feelings. She had come to love living life numb. Before she knew it, she was so deep in thought she heard Brandon calling her Dee, which brought her back to reality.

"Oh my God, why are you calling me that? My name is Diane."

"I know your name, but you need to be Dee for a while. Let me show you who Dee can be, and you decide for yourself."

"You're smug, you know that?"

He took her hand, turned and looked her square in the eye. "Let me." He kissed her hand. "Let me."

She began to feel things she hadn't felt in a very long time, and her logic battled with her emotions.

"Follow me back to my house. Let me help you relax."

"I'm not about to have sex with you."

"Who said anything about sex? Get your mind out the gutter." He chuckled. "Why everything gotta be about sex? What's wrong with you? Do you think that is all every man out here wants? Because if it is, you've been hanging out with the wrong dudes."

"So again, you mean to tell me you haven't thought one time about having sex with me?" She smirked.

That's not my motive. I truly and honestly just want to be whatever it is you need me to be right now. I know I don't know you, but I feel connected to you."

"Why? You know that's crazy, right?"

"Man, can you just live outside yourself for a minute? Trust me. I know you don't know me, but trust me. You'll never regret the day you met me. Believe that."

Diane found herself in her car following him to his house and still had no idea why she was so drawn to him. Was it because she hadn't had sex in over a year and he was this fine man who was attracted to her and made her feel things she hadn't felt in a very long time? Everything in her told her she had no business even entertaining this nonsense, after all it could go nowhere, right? But did it need to go anywhere? Could she really allow herself to just be Dee—whoever this Dee was? Was this even a possibility? Her mind was flooded with racing thoughts. Her heart began to beat rapidly, and she felt a bit panicked as he turned into a driveway and it all became real to her.

He turned his car off and jumped out, walking over to open her door. "You can just park right here behind me."

She turned the key in the ignition and pulled it out, and even though he opened the door, she just sat there still hesitant as to what to do. She was already there, but it wasn't too late to close the door, restart the car and back right out that driveway just as easily as she had pulled in. What to do? What to do? She began to panic again.

"What are you doin'? Come on."

"Here I come." She slowly grabbed her purse off the passenger seat and eased out of the car. "Alrighty, this is it, I guess."

"Man, you're crazy. Come on."

They walked up the front steps, and he unlocked the door, turning lights on as he walked in. His house was nice—nothing to the magnitude of his parents' home yet nice. When she was driving there, she didn't know what to expect, especially with his age, but it was actually really nice. She wondered if he owned it or if his parents owned it or what, but either way, it didn't really matter. She was there for one night and one night only.

"Make yourself at home. I give you free reign to do as you please. *Mi casa su casa* tonight, and for as long as you need it to be. I'm gonna go shower, but let me show you where the guest room is, and I can give you some shorts and a t-shirt if you wanna shower and relax."

"*Ummm,* yes, that would be good."

They walked through the living room to the staircase and headed up. She looked around at the different art on the walls and the overall décor. "Did your mom decorate for you, or is this all you?"

He laughed. "She helped a little, but it's mainly me."

"*Hmmm.* Good taste."

"You sound surprised."

"Well, because I am."

"Oh, wow."

They both shared a smile as he looked back at her. "Okay, here you go. The sheets and everything are clean. I'm going to grab you some clean towels and the clothes."

"Okay. Thanks." She looked around the room. There was a queen-size bed with a beautiful comforter, a sitting chair, dresser—and not a cheap dresser—and more art on the walls. It was really nice. He soon returned with her necessary items, along with lotion. He admired her admiring the pictures on the wall. He interrupted her thoughts.

"Here you go." He placed everything on the bed.

"Thanks." She was glad she was there.

Thank God, she thought as she entered the bathroom. It was spotless. She felt very comfortable. She stood under the heat of the shower escaping the day's tragedy. *This is it,* she thought, *the great escape*. She laughed out loud like a madwoman and screamed, "Yes. The great escape! The great escape." She heard a knock on the door.

"You okay in there?"

Laughing, she responded, "Yes, Brandon, I believe I'm going to be, even if I'm actually not." She talked loudly so he could hear her. "I really think I'm going to be free—free from it all. Free from me. Free from what I did. Just free."

"Okay," he answered, sounding confused. "I'm going to order Chinese. I know you might not be hungry, but I thought I would ask before I ordered."

"Just some fried rice and maybe some sweet-and-sour pork or dried fried ribs if they have 'em. Thanks!"

She stayed in the shower for almost forty-five minutes. Was she trying to wash away Diane, even if just for a little while? She toweled off and threw the shorts and t-shirt on he had left on the bed for her, then she made her way downstairs. She found Brandon in the kitchen opening up Chinese food. "Hey, mermaid. I thought I lost you."

"I was hoping to lose me."

"Well, you can. At least here you can. No judgment zone." "I wish it was that simple, Brandon. I really do." She leaned on the counter watching him take down plates and grab forks from a drawer.

"You wanna make your own plate, or would you like me to hook it up for you?"

"Thanks," she mumbled. "I can make it." She smiled a limp smile.

"Do you want to sit at the table or on the couch and watch TV or listen to music or what?"

"It doesn't matter. Maybe couch now that I think about it."

"Couch it is." They grabbed their plates, and she followed him into the living room where they ate and talked and laughed and talked and talked and talked.

Brandon caught Diane staring at him.

"What?" he said, grinning.

"Huh?" She came out of her daze.

"You're staring at me."

"No, I wasn't."

"But you were." He chuckled.

"Oh, sorry. I didn't mean to. I don't know, I was just looking at you still wondering who exactly you are."

"Who I am? Well, you won't find that out in one night. You do know that, right? Knowing someone takes time. Hey, but I'm down if that's what you're saying you want or even just need right now."

"Wait, what? What are you saying?"

"Nothing. Just that whatever you need from me—whatever that may be—I'm with it for as long as you need me to be."

"Please stop saying you can be what I need. Don't say that anymore, okay?" He nodded.

I know you are probably tired of me saying this, but we are not talking about sex, right?'

"Why do you keep bringing up sex? What is it? You have sex on the brain. When was the last time you had some?"

She threw a couch pillow at him and laughed. "Ha, you don't even want to know."

"Oh, it's like that." They both laughed.

"I wasn't necessarily talking about sex, but I'm just saying I'm here for whatever— listening, hanging out, whatever—but let me just say sex can be included if that's something you need. I mean let's just be real, we're both adults."

"*Hmmm.* Okay."

"Okay what?" He looked hopeful.

"Okay, I understand what you're saying."

"Oh, I thought you wanted sex." He started laughing hysterically. He turned on the TV and motioned for her feet. He rubbed them as she flipped through the channels before turning it off. She watched his profile as he lay his head back and closed his eyes.

"Hey, you can go to bed if you're tired. I'll be okay."

"I'm good, unless you're ready to go up."

"No. This is actually really nice. I'm just trying not to think about the fact that in a few hours I have to go back to the reality of my life."

"*Shhhh.* Leave that out there if that's going to upset you. Let this be your sanctuary."

She closed her eyes and tried to relax but couldn't help thinking about Josephine and what a mess she had made of this entire day. Her thoughts began to overwhelm her, and her heart began to beat fast. She sat up.

"I know it's getting late, and I really don't normally drink like this, but do you have any wine? I could use a glass right now."

"That's not going to fix your problem."

"Neither is sex, but you were willing to give me that."

"Whoa, whoa." He laughed. "One glass of wine coming right up. I forgot, no judgment."

He returned with wine in hand a few moments later. She thanked him and took slow, small sips over the course of the next thirty minutes.

"Do you ever think killing someone is justified?"

"Why? You thinking about killing somebody?"

"*Hmmm.* Maybe I already did."

"Girl, you haven't killed anybody." He laughed but stopped when he realized he was laughing alone. "Wait, hold on. Why are you asking me that?"

"No reason. Forget I said anything."

"Forget a woman I barely know is sitting on my couch asking me about murder justifications."

"Well, it's not like I'm going to kill you, Jesus."

"Did you kill somebody?" He was nervously intrigued.

"No. Let's change the subject."

"Oh, hell naw. That means you killed someone."

"Because I wanna change the subject? That means I killed someone? You're crazy." She leaned over and kissed him.

"Oh shoot. Yes, that's exactly what I'm saying. One minute we're talking about murder then you wanna change the subject real quick and by kissing me, Miss I'm Not Having Sex with You." He used air quotes. "You think because I'm a man I'm just gonna be like okay? Girl, you're crazy."

"Well, aren't you?"

"Aren't I what?"

"Aren't you going to say okay, Mr. I'm Going to be Whatever You Need." She used air quotes mockingly.

"Well, yeah, but as long as you don't black widow me and kill me too."

They laughed.

"You're hilarious. I don't know why we met. I think I should be scared, but I think I'm more turned on than afraid."

"That just means you have as many issues as I do."

He stood and motioned for her hand. As they walked upstairs, he stopped and turned and kissed her. It had been a long time since she had the company of a man. She melted and kissed him back with great intensity.

"We don't have to do this, you know." He looked at her.

"Yes, I know, but I want to. I need to."

As they walked up the stairs she held his hand, and she felt like the kid she was never allowed to be. She was actually a little nervous. When they got to his room, he kissed her softly and slowly, and she enjoyed every minute of it, but she knew she couldn't do this.

"Brandon, I'm sorry. I can't do this. I thought I could, but I can't."

"Hey, it's okay, Dee. Come here." He pulled her close.

"It's probably best if I just go."

"Come here." He pulled her back to the bed and motioned for her to sit down. "It's really okay." He sat back on the bed. "Here, let me just be here for you. Lay down." She lay down, and he stroked her head and kissed her forehead. "You'll be alright." He grabbed her hand, put it to his lips and kissed it, then he turned her around and held her close.

"So do you want to rest or talk?" he asked.

"Rest."

"Rest it is."

She lay there feeling safe and relaxed, but thoughts of that night began to creep into her psyche as she dozed off. Her body began to tense as she fell in and out of sleep. She saw Jim's face the night he raped her and the evil he had carried inside of him. She saw the fear in Honey's face the night she knew something had to be done. She jumped up and began pacing the floor. Brandon woke from his sleep.

"What's going on?"

"Nothing. I'm okay. I just have a lot on my mind. Go back to sleep. I'll be okay."

"Do you need me to get you anything?"

"Not unless you have a time machine or a way to rewrite history that makes me not be such a bad person. You don't know me, Brandon. Believe me. I'm a very bad person, and that's why God continues to punish me with my joke of a life. I can save everyone else's, make things better for everyone else, but never for myself."

"Do you think you're being a little hard on yourself?"

"Uh, no. Not at all. I'm being truthful with me about me."

She laid back down and tried to sleep as he attempted to comfort her, but she pulled away, saying she didn't deserve to find comfort, especially in someone as sweet and innocent as him. He didn't let it bother him. He pulled her into him and held her.

He whispered in her ear, "Everyone has a past. It matters what you do with today and the tomorrows to come."

She softened once again under his touch and relaxed enough to fall asleep, but that night she fought and sweat and whimpered, fighting demons she had fought many times before. Brandon didn't know what to make of it, but he didn't shy away. He watched her all night. He woke her when her dreams and thoughts seemed to be intense and comforted her. He wiped her head at times when the sweat showered her.

Brandon had no idea what she grappled with, but he was unrealistically bound to her for some reason.

The Bondage of Freedom

W hen a woman deserves to be free from oppression, she has to wait until the perfect opportunity presents itself and not allow her goodness to self-sabotage her destined escape. This was Diane's justification. She knew Josephine would never make a way of escape for herself, nor would she take one if it was available to her. She wouldn't return evil for evil, which was probably why Jim hated her the more. Jim wanted her to lash out, fight back and rebel at the way he treated her to help him deal with the self-hatred he had come to know so well. If she wouldn't be such a good, loving person, he could feel a little better about himself, maybe even justify his behavior, and though he would never let on, he hated the man he had become, but he was too far gone to ever come back.

He had wished sometimes Josephine would cheat or drink or be lazy, even just curse him, but she didn't. She gave him nothing while simultaneously giving him everything—her beauty, dignity, love, right down to her worth, which he took and used against her every chance he could get. Through it all, she remained the woman he married. However, Diane could only take so much. She wasn't Josephine. She rebelled, and it cost her in a major way, and one day Jim was going to pay.

It wasn't planned. Diane had thought many times what life would be like without Jim in it. Hell, they all had, and why wouldn't they? He added no value to their lives and thrived on making them feel powerless and miserable, and it wasn't fair.

Diane had come home from the skating rink with some of her friends, and she went to June's room to tell her about a boy she had met. When she opened the door, Honey was laying her head in June's lap letting out a quiet sob.

"What's wrong?" Honey looked up at June.

"Jim tried to attack her in the kitchen a little while ago."

"What do you mean attack her?" The panic set in.

"Tell her, Honey," June coaxed.

"I don't want to." Honey began to sob again.

"Somebody better tell me something." Diane began to get loud.

"Be quiet before Momma hears you," June warned.

Diane kneeled by the side of the bed and put her face close to Honey's. "You can tell me. What happened?"

Honey sat up and attempted to gather herself. She took a deep breath. "I was in the kitchen getting some juice, and Daddy came in the back door. I heard his car pull up, and I tried to hurry and put the juice away before he came in, but I just wasn't fast enough, Diane. I'm sorry."

"What are you sorry for? You didn't do anything wrong—I mean nothing, you hear me?"

She didn't have to hear the whole story to know Honey had done nothing. It was sounding all too familiar. "Go ahead."

"Well, I rinsed my glass and was leaving out the kitchen when he asked where I was rushin' off to. And I was like 'to bed' and then he grabbed my waist and said to hold on a minute. He smelled like he had been drinking, and he was acting drunk. I tried to pull away from him, and he smacked me and told me not to ever pull away from him again. I didn't know what to do. I started crying, and he told me to shut up, then he took his penis out and tried to pull up my nightgown. It was horrible, Diane, just horrible!" She began to sob and panic at the same time. Her breaths were getting short, and June and Diane tried to get her to calm down and relax.

"Then he grabbed my arm and told me I better not make a sound. I knew it wasn't right, you know, what he was trying to do, so I grabbed the telephone and hit him with it and ran upstairs to June."

June took over the conversation at this point. "She came flying in here and pushed my dresser against the door when she heard him coming up the stairs. His footsteps went to Honey's room first, and when he saw she wasn't there, he came down here. He tried to open the door, and we sat in front of the dresser holding it. He demanded we open it. He wasn't screaming because he probably didn't want to wake Momma and for her to find out the twisted demon he really is."

"You better keep your mouth shut, Honey. You hear me?" Jim spewed.

She didn't answer. She and June both just sat there up against the dresser until they heard his footsteps head back down the stairs and eventually back out the door to his car. They heard the car start and looked out the window to see the headlights reflect off the garage and eventually fade as he backed out and turned out of the driveway.

"We've been in here ever since."

"Did Momma come out?"

"No. He wasn't loud enough to wake her up. He was loud and mean and had a growl to his voice but was quiet at the same time. He hollered his whisper. I can't explain it, but he sounded like evil if evil had a voice. I hate him, Diane. I just hate him so much."

June's eyes filled with the tears of a woman who had lived a life full of torment, regret and sadness. Imagine how awful to have that kind of pain as a young woman.

"Honey, are you okay?" Diane was fuming.

"I will be okay, Diane. I was just scared, and what if he tries to do that to me again? Huh? What if the next time I can't get away?"

The dread drained all the life from her face as hers eyes welled with tears and worry about something she knew she couldn't control. It made Diane remember how she felt the night Jim raped her on the living room floor. How degraded she felt by the man who was supposed to be her father, her protector. Diane didn't allow her eyes to become teary. Instead, they filled with rage. She clinched her fist, making a solid attempt to refrain from screaming.

"Don't you worry, Honey. You'll never have to be afraid again." Diane jumped up.

"What do you mean?" Honey looked up at her full of hope, yet knowing deep down inside there was nothing Diane could ever do to stop Jim from doing what he pleased. If they learned nothing else, they had all learned that.

"I'm in the bed asleep, you got it?" Diane headed toward the door.

"What?" June looked puzzled.

"I said I'm going to bed, and I'll be there all night, okay?"

"What does that even mean?" June questioned.

"Nothing. Good night."

"Diane," June called down the hall.

Diane came back down the hall and stuck her head in the door. "Honey, you stay in here with June tonight."

"You know I can't. What if—"

Diane cut her off. "He won't. You already said he was drunk, and he's probably down at Johnny's drinking some more right now and won't even remember any of this. You'll be fine."

Diane went to her room and change her clothes. The fire for revenge burned deep inside of her like nothing she had ever felt in her entire young life. They were very protective of Honey. Jim had crossed a line of no return, and he was daring Diane to cross one as well. She looked for something she wouldn't mind disposing of. She frantically rumbled through her drawers finding a pair of sweatpants she hardly wore anymore along with a t-shirt. She dug in the back of her closet to find a pair of winter gloves.

"Perfect." She seemed pleased with the findings.

On her way out the door, she thought about needing her arms to be covered, so she grabbed her sweatshirt and threw it on. She headed quietly down the stairs, looked in the pantry, got a paper bag and a light from the drawer. Her adrenaline was high, and there was no stopping her. Once Diane had something in her head, she would follow through on it. She grabbed a knife from the wooden block that held Josephine's cooking knives, then she returned it thinking there shouldn't be a missing knife, and there was no way she could clean it, return it and allow her mother to continue to use it after it was to be used in the sinister plot she was planning. She opened the utility drawer and took a long-handled knife and dropped it in the bag.

Once outside, she jumped on her bike and pedaled as hard and as fast as she could straight to Johnny's. It wasn't that far—about a twenty-minute bike ride, but she didn't care. As she rode, she tried to figure out what she should do, and before she knew it, she was there with no plan. She rode around the surrounding block until she located Jim's car on a dark side street. She hopped off her bike and paced, trying to decide if she could go through with this and how she would do it.

After feeling like a miserable failure at her murder plot, she was set to head back home when she saw the car door was unlocked. A rush of urgency, hope and fear ran through every fiber of her being, and she knew exactly what she would do. She parked her bike on the back side of the building on the street his car was parked on, and she headed back to the car, opened the door with her sweatshirt sleeve and crouched down low in the backseat on the floor.

She waited for what seemed like an eternity, but it would be worth it. She never once battled with her connections to right versus wrong. She felt justified in what she was doing. Even when a small voice told her this was wrong, she quickly pushed it out of her head and replaced it with the look on Honey's face, the feeling of her rape and the images of her beaten mother.

Finally, nearly two hours later, she heard Jim's voice saying good night to others as he stumbled to the car singing a tune. As the tune narrowed in on her, so did the fear.

"You can do this, Diane." She encouraged herself to commit the deadly act. She balled herself up into a low, low crouch as he neared the car. He fumbled to find his key to unlock a car that was already unlocked. Finally, he pulled on the handle and let himself in.

"*Whooo,* what a night." He let out a sigh of relief.

He went to put the key in the ignition and dropped them.

"Great. Just damn great." He leaned forward and felt around for the keys. "Got 'em." As he came up and leaned back in the seat, Diane grabbed him from behind and began to stab him repeatedly in the chest. She wasn't wild and outraged. There was no need. He was so drunk he didn't even resist. She was more meticulous in her attempts not to get blood everywhere so she would have less to clean from herself.

She whispered, "This is for Honey" with the first stab. "This is for me, you sick bastard, and this is for my mother. You don't deserve her."

Jim began to gasp for air. He never felt the darkness that had come for him, but he heard Diane's painful, angry whispers, and he knew she was right. He attempted to turn to look at her to maybe give a look of sorrow and redemption, but he didn't have the strength. She watched his face through the rearview mirror as life left his body. And though it wasn't right, this one moment filled Diane as she desperately took one gasping final breath with Jim before getting out of the darkness she had just created and walking away, dragging the weight of all the women in her household.

   She paused as she got to her bike and took in her first breath of oppressor-free life for abused women everywhere. This she vowed would never happen to another woman in her house, and internally her fight for justice began that day. Never again by blood, but by the law, which was not always fair, but she knew what she had done was wrong and vowed to never play God again.

   One hour ago, she was Diane, now she was a murderer. She used her sweatshirt sleeve to turn on the water spigot where her bike rested and rinsed her hands. Right there in the alley, she undressed completely, putting back on the clothes she had worn to the skating rink and stuffing the clothes she had on into the paper bag. The only thing that really had blood on it was the sleeves of the sweatshirt and the gloves, but she wanted to get rid of it all the same. After stuffing the bag, she washed her hands again, rolled the bag up and hopped back on her bike, making sure not to ride back out onto the main street. She never even looked back at Jim, just left him there. How sad for his life to end so tragically. She rode to the park where she set the bag on fire and watched it burn until there was nothing left but the metal from the string on her sweatpants.

Back on her bike to go home. Free. She began to cry and laugh uncontrollably. She still had the knife, which she had rinsed really well. She couldn't very well put in back in the kitchen drawer. She really wanted to toss it in the lake, but the lake was too far on her bike. She finally reached her driveway and felt tired and relieved. She put her bike back on the side of the house where it had been. She couldn't really inspect it for blood as it was so dark, which she needed it to be dark. Hopefully no one saw her coming or going. Most people in her neighborhood should have been watching their eyelids long before she even left.

Quietly entering the back door, she crept up the stairs to her room, took a t-shirt from her drawer, wrapped the knife in it and tucked it between her mattresses. As she lay in bed, she made an attempt to retrace all her steps to make sure she had done everything right. She didn't want to spend the rest of her life in jail for serving up her own form of justice. She felt confident there was nothing left to tie her to Jim's murder. She didn't even touch the spigot with her hands. There were no shoe prints and no tire marks left behind, nothing. Even if there were, they would never equate it to his daughter, right? How would her mother react? Would she be pleased? Would should be sad? Mad? Diane played these thoughts over and over until she finally fell asleep right before the sun came up.

A few hours after she had fallen asleep, she was awaken by Honey getting clothes out so she could shower and get her day started.

"Hey. How are you feeling today?" Diane opened one eye looking up and over at Honey.
Honey plopped down on Diane's bed. "I didn't hear you come back last night. Where did you go?"

"I just went out for a minute to get some air and clear my head. I wasn't gone that long. You must have fallen asleep. But if

anyone ever asks you, I was here all night. Do you understand me?"
Diane mumbled but didn't look at Honey.

"*Ummm,* okay. Are you okay though? You seem a little out of
it."

"Yeah. Just tired from staying up late is all."

As Honey was standing to exit the room, June entered. "So
you sure played a disappearing act last night. Where did you go? To
find Jim no doubt." She went on. "I don't know why you let him get
to you. The best we can do is make it outta this house alive."

Diane sat up angrily in her bed. "Make it out alive? Make it
out alive?" she shouted. "Are you serious right now, June? All you
want is to make it out alive? Well, I'm sorry. I want—no, I need—
more than that. It's not fair, and I just couldn't take it anymore. How
would we ever make it out and leave Momma?"

"What do you mean you couldn't? What does that even
mean?"

"Nothing. Just leave me alone. I'm just tired and need to get
some sleep. Really, June, just leave me alone, okay? I'm not mad. I
just want to be alone, and the only place I disappeared to was this
room, got it?"

Honey and June exchanged looks, puzzled, and left out of the
room.

"Do you want the door closed?" Honey asked.

"Yes. Thank you."

In the hallway, June and Honey wondered if Diane was really
okay and if she had confronted Jim last night and if she had, if he had

done something to her to make her act the way she was. They both knew what he was capable of, but of course June knew much better than Honey, and she just hoped that wasn't the case.

And so the secret began—the secret they never wanted to believe but kept down in their hearts.

Life Keeps Moving

D iane had never fought, dreamed and relived the truth of that night as much as she did while lying in Brandon's bed. When she woke, the sun was piercing through the window blinds as she opened one eye. She then remembered where she was, and she felt Brandon's arm around her waist. She gently moved his arm, attempting not to wake him, not knowing he wasn't sleep. She sat on the side of the bed and took a deep breath.

"Hey" he said softly. "Can I get you something?'

His voice startled her. "I thought you were sleep." She didn't turn to look at him.

He scooted toward her and rubbed her lower back. She had to admit it felt nice to have someone there when she woke up.

"You had a rough night last night. Why don't you shower and I can fix you something to eat?"

"No, Brandon, you've done enough. I appreciate you. I can't keep putting you out. I need to go home and deal with my life." She turned and smiled. "Thank you. This was a lot for you to deal with I'm sure—unless you pick up random crazy women at work frequently." She smiled.

He sat up a little on his elbow and rested his head on his hand. "I would do it again for you."

"I hadn't had a night like that in a very long time, but I think it's because I was dealing with a lot of family stuff yesterday, so it was coming out in the dreams—or should I say nightmares. But I tell you, I feel free today. I feel really, really free. I could fly. Well, not technically, but you know what I mean."

She stood, and he watched her every move. She was so beautiful, and she did look different that morning. He saw the freedom she was referring to.

"I see it." He smiled.

"You see what?" She looked confused as she headed toward the door to go shower.

"I see the freedom."

"Maybe you were what I needed after all. You make me believe there is a God up there. I think you are an angel sent by him."

"Trust me, God is real. I'm not an angel, but there is a God, and he always knows what we need."

"Yeah," she said thoughtfully. "Maybe you're right."

She had begun to find her peace with what she had done. The ability to finally say out loud what she had done freed her. She didn't know what her freedom would look like or what would be facing her that day with June, but she was somehow different. While in the shower, she allowed the water to wash over and cleanse her. It was an outer cleanse that somehow she felt inwardly. There was a knock at the door.

"Hey, I ran and got you a toothbrush. Can I come in?"

"Yes."

He opened the door and set it on the sink. "You sure you don't want anything to eat?"

"Positive. Thank you."

"Okay. I'mma jump in the other shower."

"Okay."

After she pulled herself from the shower, she put on the clothes she had on the day before and headed down the stairs. She could smell bacon cooking.

"Stop trying to bribe me with bacon."

"Hey, just because you don't want to eat, I'm not going to deprive myself."

She walked over to him. She kissed him on the cheek. "Thank you again."

He knew that meant she was leaving and he was probably not going to ever see her again.

"You're absolutely sure you don't want to stay for breakfast or anything else?"

His eyes followed hers as she took a step back and looked at his shirtless chest. Every muscle in its proper place.

"I can't. As nice as I am sure it would be, I really can't." She traced his muscle with her finger. She looked up. "It was nice meeting you, Brandon." She turned and walked toward the front door.

"At least let me walk you to the door."

He watched her every step until she got into her car and drove off. He closed the front door and went to eat breakfast alone.

Once she was a few blocks away, she pulled over and took her phone out to call Richard.

He answered. "Hello"

"Richard, it's Diane. Please don't hang up. Just let me say my peace."

There was a pause. "I'm listening."

"It's probably not going to mean much, and I know they're just words, and there's no way I can't turn back time and change my actions, but I wanted to tell you I was sorry. I handled things the wrong way, and I don't know how to fix it, but I need you to know how much I love you and that I never meant to hurt you. I thought I was doing what was best for you, but I realized this morning I was just scared and didn't know how to accept the fact that I couldn't have children with you. I felt like a failure. I felt insufficient, and I thought one day you would realize it and not want me anymore. I know it sounds silly but it's my truth."

He held the phone, not saying anything.

"Are you there?" she asked.

"Yes. Yes, I'm here, just processing what you're saying. So you are calling me to apologize?"

"Yes."

"And that's it?"

"Well, can there be more?"

"I don't know. I honestly don't know, but it would be nice to hear you say something other than sorry."

She cleared her throat. What did she have to lose? "Richard, honestly, if you came back home today, I would want that, and if you said you needed to take it slow, I would accept that, but I am saying I love you, I miss you, and I decided yesterday to stop suppressing my feelings out of fear of the unknown."

"I can't believe I'm hearing this on the other end of the phone. I have never stopped loving you, and if you're serious, we can begin to work toward making this work again."

They talked for over an hour, and she smiled internally the entire time. After hanging up, she pulled back onto the road and headed toward new beginnings.

Author's Note

Many of us have secrets we bury down within, and we all deal with them differently. Some choose to deal by not dealing, simply ignoring, but no matter what, there is no doubt our experiences help shape us and mold us into the people we become, good or bad, happy or sad. A lot of times, we forget this fact, which is undeniably true, and it causes us to lose empathy for others. We never know what someone has gone through in this thing called life that has caused them to be the way they are. What I do know is that life is not for the faint of heart.

This novel enters into an unconventional direction, but my hope is to maybe, just maybe, help someone understand others as well as maybe a little more about themselves. I could easily write an ending that would encompass closure for everyone's life. Josephine could move to Atlanta or not. Diane could get back together with her ex-husband or not. Honey and Jared could live happily ever after. June could find her greater purpose and fall in love and settle down. Jim Jr. has already turned over a new leaf, and he could walk that out or go back to his old ways. The bottom line is life is unpredictable. There is never closure until we leave this earth. We could close out this chapter of their lives, but that would never tell their full story because life is fluid and is determined by the decisions we make in every moment of each day of our lives.

Jim became who he was based on the multiple incidents that transpired in his life from seeing his mother disrespected and not understanding why his father allowed it to losing the love of his life and knowing he was the reason his child was aborted. His choices in life were made based on how he allowed himself to experience life and his skewed perspective.

There was a book published many years ago entitled *Why Do Bad Things Happen to Good People?* This is an age-old question, but there is never a truly satisfying answer when you or someone you know and love are the "good" person things are happening to. What I do believe is we can choose to allow these experiences to define our entire identity, or we can choose to work through the pain of the experience and still become who we are destined to be. Oftentimes we don't know who that person is, and we aren't intentional about finding out who this person is, and therefore, we allow people, things, experiences and relationships to define us. People should never be given the authority to dictate your identity. That's too much power.

We grow, we live, we love, we feel joys and pains, and through it all, we become healthy emotionally and continue to flourish, or we become sick and sometimes get lost in a spiral of emotions that end in us making unhealthy choices, spiritually, emotionally and even physically.

My hope is the reality of this family's story will cause us to pause to realize how when we don't deal with our problems, they can manifest in a variety of different ways. Making conscious decisions as opposed to allowing life to just continue to happen takes place daily. The earlier problems are addressed, there is less likelihood of them showing up in the way they did in this family.

I am and will always be an advocate of mental health counseling because I've seen the benefits, but as it is always said, someone has to want to see something change in their lives. We may not always know what needs to change or understand the process of how to get there, but with the right support system, it's achievable.

For Believers, there is value in counseling, but there is also a place where we come to understand our identity is in Christ, and if we allow Christ to define us, we know who we are and when the circumstances of life don't align with that identity, then we must be willing to make changes, to die to self and flesh and become who we are destined to be.

Though the characters are fictitious, the reality is this could be various parts of many people's story. If you happen to identify with any of it, I hope it may give you the courage and strength to live the life you were destined to if you're not already, and if you've overcome great obstacles, remember to help someone who may not have been so fortunate. Love, empathy, understanding and support can be the difference in the path an individual takes.

As I was writing this story I had no idea I would end up here. I was simply writing a novel that may be someone's truth. The more I wrote, the more I began to think about life, the expectation of being and the experiences that create who we eventually become. I began to think about my parents, my grandparents and my great-great-grandparents and who they are and were, and how they became, and it made me realize how much we truly are products of those who were before us, good and bad.

Though the story you just read is fictional, these kinds of things the individuals lived through can happen in families all too often, but many times, there is no one there to confide in, and trauma changes us, but it doesn't have to define us. So, when life happens— and it will even to the best of us—remember you have the power to choose how you react to it.

CPSIA information can be obtained
at www.ICGtesting.com
Printed in the USA
LVHW081541160920
666190LV00018B/243/J